Into The West '98

Published by the Roscommon Herald
St. Patrick Street,
Boyle, Co. Roscommon
E-mail: roherald@indigo.ie
Tel: 079-62926

© Richard Canny and Liam Heagney, 1998
ISBN 095347240X
A catalogue record for this book is available from the British library

Printed by the Roscommon Herald,
St. Patrick Street, Boyle, Co. Roscommon

Cover photograph: Sportsfile

Into The West '98

Galway's Road To All-Ireland Success

RICHARD CANNY
LIAM HEAGNEY

Published by the Roscommon Herald

For Honor

Contents

Acknowledgements

Little did we know that a whimsical remark about writing a book on the Monday morning following the All-Ireland final would come to fruition. In hindsight, the idea bordered on lunacy considering the limitations of time.

Plenty of late nights and early mornings followed but despite it all, we have to honestly say that the enjoyment of researching and writing the book easily compensated for all the pressures.

Inevitably, there are many people to thank but it is no exaggeration to say that this book would not have seen the light of day but for the blessing of John O'Mahony. We are very grateful to John, Ger and family for their wonderful support.

To the other interviewees in the book, a sincere thank-you for your enthusiastic co-operation. Your thoughts have made this book a special memento.

Another person who must come in for special mention is Oliver Feeley, our editor, whose exacting approach to our drafts was crucial under pressure. Thanks for answering our call at such short notice. Thanks also to Adrian White of Easons for his expert advice and support from day one.

We are of course indebted to Christina McHugh, Brian Nerney and the Roscommon Herald staff for their support and work on this undertaking.

Pictures paint a thousand words and thanks to our photographers, Ger O'Loughlin, Dave Maher and his comrades at Sportsfile, Christy Regan and Mick McCormack. Thanks also to Jim Carney in the Tuam Herald for his prompt assistance.

On a personal note, deepest gratitude to our families for all their help, understanding and patience over the last month or so.

Foreword

The year was 1966. The Vietnam War, only a year old, had already burned itself onto the American consciousness; The Beatles had firmly enshrined themselves as cultural icons; Cassius Clay had adopted his new moniker 'Mohammed Ali' and the England football team sparked off wild celebrations by winning the Jules Rimet Trophy.

By 1966, Ireland was experiencing radical change on many fronts. The significant growth of an industrial base from the late fifties onwards led to the emergence of a more confident nation from the shadows of its more traditional industrial neighbours.

With the new economic climate combining with other cultural and social factors such as the advent of a home-grown television station and free education, Ireland was moving away from its image of a predominately agrarian society towards one of a modern, progressive state, absorbing the more affluent living standards of other West European countries.

It was a new vision of an enterprising nation, embraced by its people, who were enjoying the feel-good factor that the changes had generated in its slipstream. People were beginning to fasten themselves to the more realistic hopes of a prosperous future.

The huge wave of emigration that had swept through the fifties had halted and the tide had turned. Irish people were returning to their homeland, attracted by the new windows of opportunities.

1966 was the year that hurling legend Jack Lynch succeeded Sean Lemass as Taoiseach, the Fianna Fáil leader widely regarded as the economic architect of modern Ireland. That changing socio-economic fabric also came during a time when peace was the common currency in Northern Ireland.

In sport, Justin McCarthy, a precocious 21-year-old picked up All-Ireland medals at senior and U-21 level, earning him a 1966 Texaco Sportstar Award. While McCarthy was on the early cusp of a distinguished career, the legend of Galway footballing hero Mattie McDonagh was set in stone that year.

A member of the famous 'three-in-a-row' side, Mattie became the first player from Connacht to win four All-Ireland football medals. It is an achievement still unrivalled in the province to this day.

Fittingly, the Ballygar man picked up the 1966 Texaco Gaelic football award, one which came in the wake of similar honours handed out to colleagues Martin Newell a year earlier and Noel Tierney in 1964.

For all the glory that soaked Galway football during those halcyon days, however, the tail-end of that achievement marked the beginning of a long famine for football in the West. The reverberations of the three-in-a-row success soon became the vestiges of a glory that Galway and Connacht would hold on to for more than three decades. Until now.

1998 has been a watershed year for football in the West. The long, lonesome wait for Galway and Connacht football finally ended in tearful triumph last September. And within that achievement lies a fascinating, almost uncanny link with the golden years of the sixties.

Thirty two years on from the county's last football success at Croke Park, the feel-good factor is here with us once more as we enjoy another economic boom. It is a climate that is encouraging thousands of Irish people abroad to return to these shores once more. Similar also to 1966, a year that could not have envisaged the Northern atrocities that were to follow, Ireland is now experiencing the peace dividend again.

Most intriguing of all in this world of parallels, the revered tradition of Galway football has come full circle once again.

Into The West '98 is primarily about Galway winning a long-awaited All-Ireland title. It celebrates the historic victory through words and pictures; it speaks to noted figures, present and past, about its implications for Connacht football and to those who have also contributed to the '98 success. The book also reveals John O'Mahony's exclusive thoughts on the victory and looks at how the Ballaghaderreen man has developed into one of the top managers in the game.

But this book is not just a record of Galway's landmark achievement. It is an attempt to tie the nostalgic thread between the three-in-a-row heroes and the new breed of footballer in the Western province, who will now look to the future rather than to the past for confidence.

During the economic transformation of the sixties, the oft-used catch-cry was that the 'rising tide will lift all boats'. It's a description Connacht football will now undoubtedly use as a rallying cry.

1

Mission Possible

Two weekends before Mayo's second All-Ireland instalment perished on Kerry rocks, John O'Mahony was starting his own crusade with a third Connacht county. A blank canvas and a talented set of Galway players with which to mix a masterpiece. Privately, that was his ambition. Publicly, the peoples' mission statement was an All-Ireland title. Plain and simple.

With a well-documented pedigree, the anticipation of his ratification was met with much excitement, bordering on fevered in some quarters. From the early moments of his tenure, huge and somewhat bloated expectations were being foisted upon John and his raw recruits. But well-experienced in such matters, he knew the perils from the word go. Those dangers were all the more accentuated considering he was the first manager to be appointed outside the county, with the rather daunting mission of waking a sleeping giant from its slumber. It was undoubtedly his biggest assignment to date.

Basic football ability was never going to be a problem. Galway football had been reared on a diet of skill and flair but, like its Connacht neighbours in recent decades, it often came up short on the more abstract necessities of unswerving self-belief and confidence. In the face of such strong tradition and with the glory days of the sixties still the mirror in which current achievements would be compared, it was a big managerial gamble. John, however, needed little guidance in assessing the potential of a team backboned by promising raw talent and precocious youth. All that was missing from the collage was mental steel.

It was a challenge he could not ignore and within a short space of time, the players soon began to hum to his mantra of positive thinking. One of the original inter-county managers to delve into the area of mental conditioning, John, before it ever became fashionable, looked destined to be drawn towards the benefits of positive thinking. A man who preached the calm and composed gospel, it was never fists through the table stuff.

As a secondary school student at St. Nathys College, Ballaghaderreen in the early to mid-eighties, my own memories of John training the juvenile colleges team that I was once part of are vague. There are no vivid recollections of any of the team-talks. There are no specific images of players hanging on his every word. All I can remember is a picture of a man whom I cannot recall ever using bile-inducing rants on the sideline or in the dressing-rooms. The broad brushstrokes of my mind paint a picture of a calm figure never ruffled whether in defeat or victory. Now looking back and forward simultaneously, my perceptions of the man are continuous: he has unconditional respect for and awareness of his players.

That emphasis on the mental conditioning is touched on in an interview I conducted with him in the weeks leading up to the All-Ireland final. "In general terms, being a manager, it is important that he sends out the right body language and doesn't send out the wrong vibes. If he's panicking on the sideline, players see that panic and that transfers itself immediately to them. In terms of a management style, it's better to project the cool positive image. It's up to others to decide whether I do that or not."

His Galway brief was to turn a bunch of different but very able individuals into winners. The central figure he may have been but there was no regimented or military-like division between master and subjects. Similar to the teams he was involved with in the past, he got to know each one individually. It wasn't just their merits as a footballer. It wasn't just the organisational stuff that would lead to contact with his charges. It wasn't just the *craic* and banter on the training ground. It didn't stop there. It became very personal.

Not surprisingly, embracing the role in a very personalised fashion is becoming increasingly demanding and John predicts that inter-county managers will become full-time within the next decade. "I can see a situation in ten years time, after I'm totally finished with it, that an inter-county senior team manager will be a full-time employee of the County Board. I think it is right and the way it has to go. You have full-time secretaries of provincial councils and you have the same with some County Boards. They are doing a tremendous job and the G.A.A. is better for it. I don't see any conflict down the road with people taking a few years off from their job to take over teams. I have no vested interest because it won't come in my time so I'm not trying to promote this."

In his contact with players, John wants to know them not just as inter-county footballers but as human beings who are inter-county footballers. It is a central feature of a successful philosophy. A team is a motley crew, comprising players of varying social and career backgrounds. The big task is injecting harmony into that mix. Pull on the jersey and everyone's equal, no matter what the background or circumstance. Pull on the jersey and make sure everyone is singing from the same hymn-sheet. Not an easy task but it is a nurturing approach that he has always espoused.

"You use the carrot stick approach and that's where the man-management side of things come in. You become caught up in the personal lives of players - sometimes people wonder if you are a counsellor or a team manager. But it's hugely important and you want to know the environment where players come from and the difficulties they have maybe at work or at home. You have to get into the nitty-gritty of their home life because you want to create a right atmosphere for them. If somebody comes out from the house where somebody is sick or has lost their job or maybe didn't have a job and you shout at them at training...I think once you know the background, you might approach the thing in a totally different way."

His style is one that warrants personal journeys from the players and not surprisingly it is delicate territory. The emphasis, however, is very much on the player wanting to respond to the promptings. "I think the best way of doing this is to create the 'want' in the person to do something rather than enforce anything on them. There are dangers fraught in all of that but if you get that great want, he will naturally say 'how do we do this then?'. People talk about things like managers demanding respect and being close to the players, so you're walking a thin line. For some players, you can get very close to them because they know you're trying to get the best out of them. One of the things you are always looking for in somebody is 'does it really mean anything to them?'. If it doesn't, then you're in trouble straightaway."

This year's national league was used as a testing ground for his objective of moulding a team together for the championship. The rumblings of a growing team collective grew ever louder when the team, after clinching promotion, reached the quarter-finals where Offaly lay waiting to check that momentum. That defeat showed there was still tinkering to be done in a number of sectors but the confidence on the terraces in advance of more important summer challenges remained undimmed. For John, there was an extra and unplanned edge added to his work. The quest for a Connacht title was to be a journey strewn with emotional debris. Apart from the gruelling games against Roscommon in the final, the 1998 Connacht championship eventually took its toll and characteristically, he dealt with most of that pressure privately. His previous connections with two other Connacht teams were to turn the provincial campaign into an extremely personal journey for him. The first round game against the provincial title-holders, Mayo, in Castlebar set the benchmark for the rest of the campaign.

"This year we played two teams that I have formerly managed and I found that difficult. Mayo is my native county and a lot my personal friends are from the county and I support Mayo. Some of the players that I managed were still playing and they are still my personal friends. In that sense, you have to see the bigger picture and you hope everybody sees it as well."

The diktat of professionalism is ever-present. A job still has to be done and whatever of the heart-felt emotion, the business of winning is still observed meticulously. Other intense feelings had to be veiled not for the first time in his managerial career. "You have to be as professional as possible. You divorce the heart-strings from the job you're doing. Anyway, you become emotionally involved with the team you're involved with. It was difficult though with Mayo this year. You had a team that was in two All-Irelands and should have won an All-Ireland, and I was involved in their downfall. I think though that people are big enough to appreciate the bigger picture.

"My time with Leitrim was also very good - the tremendous memories I have of some of those guys in the few years I was with them. It was a difficult and emotional day for me in Carrick-on-Shannon this year and particularly because of the fact we beat them well. Then we had Roscommon in which I was involved deeply in club football last year. I would already have been involved with a lot of the people in that county but the friendships were embellished last year. So, I found the experience in the championship with Roscommon difficult as well."

The personal dimension inevitable in the provincial campaign and the snowballing expectations were features that many felt led to some uncharacteristic public emotion after finally dismantling Roscommon's resilience in the Connacht final replay. I wrote as much in the *Roscommon Herald* about O'Mahony the week after that game. "Composure has always been a strong quality of John O'Mahony's but even the white heat of battle proved his undoing. The Galway manager was as emotionally charged as the milieu that embraced him."

His usually measured thoughts gave way to feelings that ordinarily he would have kept a lid on. Speaking to the *Herald* after the game, the vetting mechanism inside his mind tripped and the words flowed. "There was a lot of things said about our team in the last fortnight since the drawn game. There was expectancy probably from some people - there's a lot of kids out there, and that's the way I look at them. There was a lot of learning to do but it was unreal expectation and we came and did a lot of learning out there on the field today.

"We were passed the favourites tag over the last few weeks and people would have said that we wore it uneasily. There were a lot of things written about us in the national media, in particular the day after the drawn game, and that got us going a little bit. We know we have to improve but the very people who put us up on a pedestal will knock us down at the end of the day. We have to keep an even keel..."

That emotion was also very evident in an *R.T.É.* interview he gave moments after the final whistle. Weeks after, he has some interesting reflections on that day. "I got a lot of slagging about that T.V. interview. There was a great sense of relief after that game. At the end, there was a lot of passion and a release of tension. I was absolutely drained after that match. The farther you go in this game, the longer one is involved, everyone wants to be as successful as they can. I suppose everyone is developing and I would be as a manager in the sense that we beat Mayo and Leitrim and there was a lot of pressure on us. There was an unreal atmosphere in some respects. That Leitrim result might have set Leitrim back but it set us back as well. I was annoyed - not annoyed but it was the build-up of the Galway team after the first two games.

"We were down from ten-to-one to six-to-one with the bookies to win the All-Ireland and were just heading into a Connacht final. I would have said at the time that there were a lot of things we would need to improve on here and we're a young team and all the rest of it. And yet people did not listen. Then, of course, the team was questioned after the drawn match in Tuam. I felt people maybe should have been questioning themselves about their assessment. I would have realised that we'd have played way below our potential in the first match and that fortnight before the replay was more pressurised. The initiative switched to Roscommon a little bit and we had to try and get things back on track. But it was a great experience for the young lads in particular to carry the burden of favouritism so heavily."

It must be emphasised though that while the veil may have slipped a little, his dressingroom after that replay, like previous and subsequent Galway dressingrooms last season, reflected not the expected unbridled emotion but an oasis of eerie calmness. Despite his animation that day, his influence was clearly having an enormous effect.

My colleague, Liam Heagney, in the *Herald's* edition that week, captured that unique picture of a Galway dressingroom that should have been gushing on winning only a second provincial title since the turn of the decade: "Winning dressingrooms, at the best of times, usually tend to be a heaving mass of humanity. Fans loitering, ready to back-slap players, media looking for words of wisdom from glorious warriors, and County Board personnel mingling and bathing in the reflected glory of their side's success. Not so at Hyde Park. The Tribesmen's inner sanctum was a picture of calm. Then again, it was calm, and locked, in Tuam after the draw."

The scoreline in the subsequent All-Ireland semi-final against a limited Derry side may not have reflected the dominance of Galway but of all the big games over the season, it was the one where his team finally began to substantiate some of the more ambitious expectations. It was a satisfying experience for everybody concerned. And maybe more so for John than anybody. He had negotiated the minefield of Connacht, there was no baggage associated with the semi-final and the lads went on to perform impressively. No personal thoughts or emotions were in danger of being unveiled and there was no rationalisation to be done. Things were back on track.

Galway played extremely well against a Derry team that not only withered in a sea of maroon but disintegrated on a counter-productive short passing game. John reflects on that game without any crease on his brow. "I suppose the fact that we struggled to win in Connacht was a help psychologically. Before the Derry game, I think the squad felt that we had a great chance of winning. A lot of the team, seven or eight of them, were there in '95 where they ran Tyrone to a few points. We felt that we had the Derry game fairly well-analysed and we felt confident of victory. Having said that, I thought we would have got a stronger fight from Derry. There was a great feeling of satisfaction afterwards."

The words of caution he preached in the teeth of huge expectation since the beginning of the campaign had now even begun to filter through to the supporters. There was the usual hype associated with the weeks leading into an All-Ireland but John felt that the Galway faithful had not hindered preparations.

People had been allowed to watch the players go through their paces in the alternate venues of Tuam and Ballinasloe but in the final weeks, there was no excessive hype hampering preparations. He expressed that satisfaction in advance of the game. "There is an expectancy and a buzz around the place but I have to say I'm quite pleased with the level of realism, allowing us to get on with the job up to now."

Not as personal as the Dublin coverage in 1995 perhaps, but Kildare, after their Leinster triumph, had become the darling of the Dublin media. They provided good copy in an instant - they had smashed the Leinster monoliths; they had beaten the last three All-Ireland winners; their pacey, leg-pumping, short passing game revived some of the dash of the seventies and eighties' Kerry teams; they had reached their first All-Ireland final since 1935 and perhaps their most publicised clarion call was Brian Lacey's outgunning in the championship of three of the most celebrated players in the modern game, Jason Sherlock, Tommy Dowd and Maurice Fitzgerald.

In the run-up to the final, I asked John did he have a preference on the outcome of the Kildare-Kerry All-Ireland semi-final. It became clear in his reply who he thought were being pinned as favourites for the Sam Maguire. "I had no preference on the outcome of the other semi-final because there would be attractions in both teams. If it was Kerry, it would be because they were All-Ireland champions and so on and we would be the novel team. The fact that Kildare have now beaten the last three All-Ireland champions means we won't be carrying the baton of favourites. We're looking forward to the prospect of playing Kildare - both teams like to attack the ball, they are new teams. They're fresh and hungry. I think Kildare are an excellent team. They have shown on this year's performances that they have a tremendous work ethic and a tremendous sense of teamwork. They seem to be mentally stronger than they have been in the past in the sense that when they lost Niall Buckley, it didn't affect them. Their fitness and workrate is huge and it's going to make it a huge task.

"Kildare have the credentials and probably have had a lot harder road than we have had. Looking at some of the comments nationwide, Kildare are the favourites. The feeling I'm getting is that they have their name on the trophy. In the run-up to this game, I would say that it's within our possibility to win this if certain things are done and I certainly feel we have a chance of winning this All-Ireland."

In that particular interview, he is also asked about the ghosts of 1966, the last time Galway and a Connacht team took Sam west of The Shannon. The question is approached in a very decisive manner. "In terms of historical baggage and the fact that a Connacht team has not won an All-Ireland since 1966, I think in fairness to the Galway culture, I don't think it is something that there is a huge consciousness or fear of." In the next breath, he reveals his ambassadorial duties for football in the West. With many friendships throughout the province, he took strong cognisance of the fact that the whole of the province was behind him. No ghosts of yesteryear haunted this man.

"I would not see representing Connacht on All-Ireland day as a burden. I'm proud to carry the banner. The support for teams from the West in Croke Park - that's a conscious thing over the last few years since the trauma of Mayo in '93. Things dipped a lot but there's been great support for Connacht teams in Croke Park, even for minor teams. A great Connacht thing is there now and there is good camaraderie among people from the province in Croke Park."

That font of goodwill from other counties and from local people in his home town of Ballaghaderreen was a feature at the forefront of his mind in the countdown to Croke Park. "The local support has been fantastic. I would highly respect the Roscommon and Mayo supporters in Ballaghaderreen. Some of them came to our hotel after the Derry game. When I took up the Galway job, there would have been some Mayo people who would have felt that I was going to the real enemy. But it's been amazing the amount of well-wishers from Mayo and Leitrim and from players and officials who have phoned to wish us well."

The backdrop of well-wishers is a characteristic he was obviously conscious of but he had to balance that excitement with the need to keep his players calm and focussed. Narrowing the thoughts on the game in the weeks beforehand was the antidote to the rising level of excitement among Galway people but, in that conundrum, he is also aware of the importance of that support. He told me then that his plans would inevitably be set against the backdrop of the All-Ireland gravy train.

"Obviously the immediate thing is the 3.30 pm. throw-in. You work your preparations into that and everything is geared towards that. There is obviously a lot of sideshows coming up to the All-Ireland. There are ways and means of trying to deal with that - not to insulate it or pretend it's not there. But there are ways of mentally preparing for that. On All-Ireland day though, we will let the team coach come through the supporters, the flags, the whole lot. It's great for the players, they realise that the whole county is behind them."

On September 27th, the dark cloud hovering over football in the West finally lifted. The black Connacht nightmare that had long enveloped Croke Park turned into a wonderful technicolour dream. On that Sunday evening, at about five o'clock, Ray Silke's oration banished the bad old days, and the exorcism of past disappointments was completed by a blanket of maroon and white singing a few rousing bars of 'The Fields of Athenry'. The mind-numbing joy of it all had hairs standing on a thousand napes. All the maelstrom of emotion, pain, memories, long nights, sacrifices - compressed into and erased after seventy minutes of heart-warming football.

Connacht football in terminal decline. That was the view of many up to recent years after decades of devastating defeats and depressing journeys home from Croke Park. But no more! Galway's wonderful victory is like the sensation of drawing the curtains back on a dark and musty room and allowing the sunlight to fill every corner. So often punters have bemoaned the wretched displays of Connacht teams at G.A.A. headquarters. That Sunday not only answered the critics and detractors in clinical fashion but Galway, reviving the classical tradition of direct football, go down in history as one of the few teams that won the Sam Maguire in wonderful fashion. Apart from a series of memorable individual displays, this is a victory for the team collective with O'Mahony and his trusty selectors, Stephen Joyce and Peter Warren at the helm.

There is a very appropriate ending to my experiences of the Galway manager over the course of the campaign. Inadvertently, I bumped into John on the streets of Ballaghaderreen in the days running up to the game. We naturally talked about the All-Ireland but in the course of the conversation, he became aware that I was having difficulty in getting a pass for the Croke Park press box.

In the middle of the pitch amid a throng of people and less than an hour after a watershed All-Ireland title, he casually asked me whether I had managed to secure press accreditation. Placed out of context, this particular story may seem bland. But when a man who had just unshackled a thirty two-year-old ball and chain around Galway and Connacht football remembers a conversation he had earlier in the week, then that gives some indication of what a composed level of reality John O'Mahony operates on.

"Did you get into the...(press box)," he nodded. "Yes," I said. "Good man, good man," he replied.

Our meeting after the game materialised after I had nabbed him for a few words. As accommodating as ever, he made time for the interview, all the more admirable considering he had just finished a few rounds with the T.V. and radio people. He was a remarkable temple of calm. Submerged by a sea of emotion, I had managed to catch his attention amongst the well-wishing chaos of men, women, children and babies. At that time, he was making his way back to the dressingrooms, located within the bowels of the Cusack Stand. How do you feel, John? Do you feel emotional?

"No, I feel relaxed and there's a nice relaxed feeling. We needed that to win this - a calmness. The last big team tactical talk was last Wednesday night. There was very little said all weekend. We had been preaching the message all year. Really, the weekend was about calmness and about relaxation. To win an All-Ireland is a fantastic feeling but it really has not sunk in yet."

In view of the first half which had swung decidedly in favour of Kildare, I asked him how did he change it around at half-time? "I did not change it, they changed it on the field. We got the early start but in the second part of the first half, we were not getting the ball in as quickly as we would have liked. Now part of that was the wind actually but it looked as if there was no wind out there. In the second half, once we were getting it in direct, I knew we were in business."

During the mid-pitch interview, a smile of satisfaction lit up his face when he was reminded of some of the scintillating football in the first quarter of the second half. "That was the turning point of the game really. All through the game today, there were people who had sticky patches but each one of them at particular times did magnificent things. So it was a team victory for the sixteen that played and the fourteen that did not play, and all the people behind us."

How did he feel as a Connacht man at that very moment? "Fantastic in the sense that Galway brought it back. But it's a victory for Galway first of all and a victory for Connacht. And I think all the other teams, particularly Roscommon - Roscommon in the Connacht final made this team, I believe, as Mayo did."

The calm, controlled mind inevitably turned to old stomping grounds. "Leitrim had a bad time this year but next year they will all be there. I think it was the extra competitiveness we have had in Connacht in the last few years...that has finally made the breakthrough. Mayo in the last couple of years had been so close. We're the lucky ones that have made the breakthrough now. You never know who is going to be winning the All-Ireland. I hope it's from Connacht next year."

A diplomat to the very core, the interview ended with consolatory words for the vanquished. "They're fantastic ambassadors. They came under the same psychological pressure today that we probably came under in the first Connacht final. We were delighted the way we came into today's game but Kildare will be back, there's no doubt about that." With that, the temple of calm was absorbed into a whirlpool of undiluted joy.

With a talented and disciplined bunch of players, John O'Mahony has reached the summit of his managerial career by maximising that talent through tactical and organisational brilliance. What makes the man such a perfect role-model for aspiring managers is that he always approaches his work with commendable humility.

John O'Mahony has become the modern day football alchemist. Experimenting with the raw ingredients of talent in the pursuit of success. Unlike those mediaeval charlatans, however, much of what he touches has turned to gold. Over the last decade, he has become the touchstone in the fortunes of Connacht football. First it was Mayo's fruitless but inspiring All-Ireland adventure in 1989 which generated a huge surge on the national credibility chart.

Next up was Leitrim who no longer were the poor relations after their historic breakthrough in 1994. Now it is his achievement of waking the slumbering giant of Galway football and sweeping them to All-Ireland glory. And in succeeding in reviving the ancient arts of the catch, kick and long-range shooting, he has provided the worthy link with the three-in-a-row team of the sixties.

For other mortals, being the moving spirit behind such achievements would be dizzying. For John, there is no arrogance. There is no attention-seeking. Just a quite sense of satisfaction at a job well done and completed by a devoted group of people. It is a feeling at odds with a career that is positively dripping with milestones.

From the very beginning of his odyssey with senior teams in the Western province, his cool style of management has caught the attention of punters, the public and aspiring managers everywhere. An aura and even a mystique surrounds the football addict whose understated but masterful authority has guided teams out of the shadow into a new era.

What makes his style of approach much studied is the fact that he is not wont to discuss the magic formula openly with the media at large, which have come to view his stock remarks with a sense of helplessness. They seek for what lays beneath but all they ever find is a man who is always accommodating but never revealing. It's not that John covets his thoughts and abilities away from broader scrutiny like a churlish child. It's simply to do with the fact that much of his approach comes from within.

He is a master motivator - looking into the souls of players, filling them with confidence and self-belief and receiving unconditional loyalty and dedication in return. It is a style that warrants personal journeys from the players and not surprisingly, it is sacred territory - territory that laid the foundations for a watershed All-Ireland title and knowing John, that territory will remain sacred.

2

The Comeback Kid

If you can keep your head when all about you
  Are losing theirs and blaming it on you,
If you can trust yourself when all men doubt you,
  But make allowance for their doubting too;
If you can wait and not be tired by waiting
  Or being lied about; don't deal in lies,
Or being hated; don't give way to hating
  And yet don't look too good nor talk too wise.

                              If - Rudyard Kipling 1865-1936

Somehow the above extract from Kipling sums up the player that is Martin McNamara. Singled out as a root of defensive weakness which sent Galway packing in the first round of 1997's Connacht championship, Martin gave leeway to those that doubted but kept his head, and scaled the All-Ireland heights last March with Corofin and last September with Galway. And yet, through it all, he maintains an engaging disdain for his own importance. Personification indeed of Kipling's literary musings.

May 1997 was a time not remembered with any great sentimentality by the goalkeeper, known to all as Mac. Mayo had swaggered into Tuam and Mac played his part in handing them a first heist at the North Galway venue for forty six years. Mistakes led to the concession of sloppy scores and the keeper became the focus of much merriment from the massed Mayo ranks behind his goal. The newspapers were equally cutting in their assessments the following morning. One daily bugle made reference to a comment from a Galway player who had boasted the Friday before the Mayo clash that Martin McNamara 'could land a ball on a five pence piece in the middle of the field'. Come the Monday, the scribe relayed that the goalkeeper 'had difficulty in hitting human targets infinitely bigger than shilling bits in a much shorter range'. It was a caustic analogy but it was indicative of the general consensus.

Normally unfazed by such events, the underachievement against Mayo affected Mac in a manner he had not experienced previously. Coping with the disappointment became a real distraction. Such were the repercussions he even reached the stage where he contemplated scaling down his playing activities. Luckily for Galway, close friends of Mac's steered him towards the path of rediscovery and his confidence was gradually rejuvenated. "My confidence was shattered after the Mayo one. I made a couple of mistakes and every time a mistake was made we were punished. We only lost by four points in the end, but I was probably the cause of 1-3. We made more stupid mistakes out the pitch as well so we probably gave away about 1-5 or 1-6, silly scores really which we shouldn't have given away.

"The thing against Mayo really got to me all right. Normally it doesn't bother me. Most days I play football for the *craic* you know, a few pints afterwards and whatever. But last year, it hit me in a different way. I was probably stupid enough, I let it get to me too much. But I'm over that. I was going to forget about it all right. I was going to stop playing. But a couple of guys - Pat Comer, he was sub goalkeeper this year, Gay Mitchell and of course my own club mates at home in Corofin - they all helped me forget about it. When you think about it, it's only a game."

Confidence is the healthiest of all infections and in a bid to come under its influence, Mac wintered well with Corofin, playing his part as they won their third ever Connacht club title. A sole national league appearance, ironically against Mayo in a drawn encounter at Castlebar last November, initiated his rehabilitation in the county colours. But with Pat Comer the preferred number one, Mac had to wait until the league quarter-final in April against Offaly, a couple of weeks following Corofin's tumultuous All-Ireland club win, to stake a claim for a championship starting slot against Mayo. That place was granted, helped by a lingering groin injury carried by Comer, and 29-year-old Mac never looked back.

"Playing club football helped build up my confidence again gradually. The guys out in Corofin, they brought me on really and as games went on and we kept winning things were going right for me. It got back to normal again, so that helped. Only for Pat Comer having a groin strain I don't think I would have been in goal at all for Galway. There was a lot of pressure on me personally going up to Castlebar because you would always have the guys behind the goal saying 'kick it short' and jibing you and whatever. But it was brilliant. I made a mistake earlier on, but lucky enough, things went right for me after that. It was a personal triumph as well as a team one."

There followed a string of fine individual performances, decorated with some vintage shot-stopping that kept Galway in the hunt in pressurised times. In particular, the pair of first half saves to deny Roscommon's Lorcan Dowd and Tommie Grehan certain goals in the Tuam Connacht final stood out. Mac then brought his agility to Croke Park to frustrate Derry but come All-Ireland final time, the national media jury was still out and deliberating on Mac's worthiness. The accuracy of his kick-outs was under scrutiny. Not that Mac minded. "They were probably judging that on the Mayo game last year. I couldn't complain about that either. If I was watching from the sideline, looking at this guy kicking the ball out last year, I'd say it was a definite weakness too."

September 27th marked the conclusion of Mac's epoch, a season that delivered two All-Irelands. It was swift elevation to a much praised plateau, a turnabout he took in his stride. Not one to get above his station, he appraises his own achievements with characteristic modesty. The trappings of fame are not for him. "I wouldn't look at myself as anything special, but I remember when I used see the Galway players when I was young, they were Gods to me. So I would appreciate the way the kids would be looking up to me. It's nice to have a young guy, a young kid coming up and asking 'sign this for me, Martin'. Six months ago they wouldn't have a clue who you were. It's a nice turnaround. And a year ago they would have been asking me if I wanted their autograph. Some guy said to me as well 'you should go for election' so I turned around to him and said 'if I went for election last year my own father and mother wouldn't vote for me'."

Possessing a firm insight to the polar extremes experienced in an evolving sporting life, Mac counts himself as a player decreed with a great deal of good fortune. After all he had grown up in an era when great players, favourites of his like Tony McManus, Dermot Earley and Val Daly, were left bereft of the most desired accolade. "I wouldn't complain if I never won it again. When you look at the likes of Tony McManus of Roscommon who hasn't won an All-Ireland medal and you have an auld gouger like me having two of them, it makes you appreciate it. It makes it mean so much more. I wouldn't lace the boots of those players, to be honest with you."

One final tale, originating from his schools days at the St. Jarlaths footballing academy, puts 1998's rich streak in Mac's career into perspective. "When I was in Jarlaths, Paul Staunton was keeper. He went on to become the Roscommon keeper for a while. I was sub on the Jarlaths team for about two matches the year they won the All-Ireland final, but I had not a chance in the world of getting in instead of him so I started playing soccer. Now I've got the All-Ireland medal. But if Paul was lucky enough to be from Galway, I would have been up in the Hogan Stand looking at him last September. The same could go for another amount of players as well. I'm going to enjoy it as much as I can."

Just as Kipling had written in *If*, Mac, regardless of his triumphant year, ensures he neither looks too good or talks too wise.

*   *   *   *

Corofin lies approximately six miles from the pull of the big lights of Tuam. Like many villages in rural Ireland under the influence of a nearby, densely populated town, people naturally migrate to the bigger place. Its lure does not need explaining. Martin himself is now a publican in charge of *McNamaras* in Tuam. Such migration leaves Corofin and other villages largely dependent on the activities of the G.A.A. to give them a real identity. That pride in the parish becomes especially vivid on every St. Patrick's Day when the All-Ireland club championship finals are held at Croke Park. With participants revelling in the limelight the occasion induces, those finals are now one of the most awaited dates on the G.A.A's. annual calendar.

Pride in one's parish has been particularly strong in Corofin of late. Blessed with the dedication of great clubmen such as Frank Morris who trained the minors to five county titles in a row, prowess on the playing field was just as evident amongst the senior ranks. County champions four times already this decade, Connacht titles were won in both 1993 and 1995. A third success was theirs in 1997, and this time they went on to introduce themselves to the big club day out in Croke Park.

Although their opponents Erin's Isle were a side that equally thrived on its community background, Corofin's desire for an All-Ireland was that bit greater. The significance of the win is not lost on Mac. "It was brilliant out in Corofin because it is a rural area. There's absolutely nothing else to do only football, so it meant quite a bit winning it out there. Football's a huge part of the lifestyle. Growing up out in Corofin, I went to the national school and everything centred round the G.A.A...there was Scór na nÓg, the talent competition, and football. If you didn't do that you went playing pool in the pubs. You tried to play pool as well but mostly it was football. I used to play at corner-forward up until U-14s. Then when everybody else grew up to be the same size as me I was useless, so they shoved me back into the goal. I was not happy at the time, but when I realised I wasn't going to get a place outfield I was happy enough with it." Satisfied with the position of custodian, Roscommon's Gay Sheeran, Galway's Gay Mitchell and Kerry's Charlie Nelligan became players of that era who were influential in honing

Mac's own goalkeeping style, a shot-stopping talent that was to flower under the national spotlight.

"A lot of Connacht teams had gone to Croke Park and they were good enough to win, but just didn't go out and grab it. Corofin showed the rest of us. They were not a super team - there were no brilliant individuals - but they were a good team and played as a team. That showed the way for Galway as well. If you can go out as a team, you can beat anybody.

"Corofin had won Connacht twice before and we knew that the two previous times we won the team was young. Even last year, the guys were still only twenty five or twenty six, so they were still in their prime. We knew they were still good enough to go on and win Connacht again. But to win an All-Ireland you need a lot of luck, so you can't take anything for granted.

"We had a lot of luck. In all the club championship games one of the other team's stars was missing nearly all along. That helped us. In the All-Ireland semi-final against Dungiven, one of the Dungiven guys was sent-off. That afforded us to leave two guys on Joe Brolly. That was a stroke of luck. And against Erin's Isle then, Charlie Redmond was sent-off so he was missing as well. He was a crucial part of their team. We had the rub of the green all year."

That rub of the green was deserved, especially as Tuam acts as the centre of football in Galway. Its hinterland contains a high concentration of clubs, including Corofin, and their continuing eagerness to be the best has led to a surge in the standard of football in recent years. "There's nothing else but football. Most of the people involved in those clubs would come into Tuam. You would know each other and when you would go out and play each other the rivalry would be pretty sticky at times. That has helped to bring on football in the last couple of years."

With survival in that rarefied atmosphere hard-earned, Corofin built on it to ensure national success poured forth. Celebrations were unprecedented in the village, with Mac's family especially pleased. "My mother and father, they never had a Gaelic background themselves. My older brother Pat, he played for Jarlaths and won a Hogan Cup. He was helping me a lot down the years. Mike, my other brother, he played a bit of football up to junior level. His heart and soul were in it. So they helped a lot down the years. Me winning both All-Irelands has probably meant more to them than it has to me. They've been like kids over it - thrilled!"

Such is the wondrous quality called pride in the parish.

*   *   *   *

The intrinsic amateur ethos of the G.A.A. has been a characteristic that has magnified the sport's widespread appeal. Like everyone else, players have day jobs to see to before they grab their kit bags and head off to training grounds the length and breadth of the country. Pillars of the community, their footballing ability is forever appreciated. An aspect of that appreciation is the exodus of players abroad to America every year to live there for a while and play football with the local clubs. Having noted footballers in their ranks is a feather in the cap of all American clubs. And Martin McNamara's affiliation in 1994 and 1995 with the Connemara Gaels club in Boston was no different.

With inter-county football for Galway of secondary importance at the time, despite making a championship debut away to London in 1994, Mac summered Stateside two years in a row. There, football was the weekend release following strenuous weekdays on the building sites. Working for two Italians who constantly mounted up the hours no matter whether the sun was splitting rocks or the rain was teeming down, Boston was a place where you worked hard and partied often. "I went out to play with Connemara Gaels. I knew one of the guys, Roger Kiely. He played with them, so he invited me to go out. I just stayed for six months at first and I came back home for the winter. I went back out there the following year, again for six months. '94 was the first year I went out. I actually played with Galway, and when we got beaten by Leitrim I went to America straightaway. The following year I went to America in April, so I missed the whole season. Galway actually won the Connacht final that year, so I thought there was a little message there for me to actually stay away."

But self-imposed exile was never likely to happen. The lure of home was too much to ignore. "Nearly fifty to sixty per cent of people involved with the Connemara Gaels were from Galway. It was really a home away from home. It was o.k., but there's no place like Galway to be honest with you. You could afford a better standard of living all right in Boston, but the *craic* around here with your friends and family - there's no comparison, really."

Back amongst his own, football re-established its grip on Mac. 'Bosco' McDermott was in charge of Galway in 1996 and Mac was soon drafted into the panel as cover for Cathal McGinley, the incumbent between the sticks at the time. It was a selection that rekindled an involvement which led to All-Ireland success two years later. Change was also afoot in Mac's personal life. Having dallied in a variety of employments, he eventually decided to take the plunge during summer 1998 and become a publican. It was a decision that brought stability to his working responsibilities and created optimum time to meet the commitment demanded of modern day inter-county football. "I was all over the shop for a couple of years. I like a bit of *craic*. I like a good time, to be honest with you. I'd been in America, I'd been in England and I had worked in Galway for about five years. When I came back from America, I worked in Galway again driving an auld truck. My brother owned the bar here in Tuam. It was up for lease, so I decided to have a go at it."

Little did he realise back then that *McNamaras*, instead of being run by an inter-county footballer, was on the verge of becoming a public house run by an All-Ireland winner.

*   *   *   *

An increasing competitiveness within Gaelic football has evolved during the nineties. No longer are realistic All-Ireland ambitions the monopoly of the elite few. Genuine designs of glory are harboured by many and as winter lurched into the summer of 1998, more than a dozen counties went to post intent on realising their hopes. Galway were one of the contenders. Provincial champions in 1995, they had subsequently made successive exits to Mayo, back-to-back winners in Connacht and unfortunates in back-to-back All-Ireland finals. Pedigree suggested that Galway were bordering that fine line which divided winning and losing and the sages had it that provincial success was very much within their compass. Cherry-picking a Connacht triumph though would be no easy feat. The nineties' provincial playground had become a competitive jungle where all teams were capable of beating each other.

Martin McNamara, for one, recognises this metamorphosis. "It has balanced out incredibly. For years in Connacht there was always one or two teams that dominated. You would maybe have two easy games in Connacht and go out playing the Leinster champions or someone like that, and you wouldn't have any games really going up to it. Not in my time now. That was a huge disadvantage to Connacht teams, but the past few years there has been no easy game. Mayo were up there in Croke Park and could have won two All-Irelands. Because they have had hard games all along in Connacht probably brought them on."

Despite this additional competitive edge to games within the province, Mac ventured out at the beginning of the season in the belief that a Connacht title was the sole realistic goal within Galway's reach. Back then, Jarlath Fallon, Tomás Mannion and Kevin Walsh were absent from Galway's equation, vital players who were, on their returns, to prove the missing links in the All-Ireland winning squad. "Without those three players I thought

Galway would be in serious trouble. I wasn't taking away from the other players. They're all very good as well, but those guys were experienced and nothing seemed to bother them. They were great leaders. Tomás Mannion at corner-back was a revelation. He was always a brilliant player with Galway but never got the praise he deserved. He was one of the best players in Ireland for years. Kevin Walsh was a big addition when he came back and strengthened the middle of the field. Seán Ó Domhnaill is only a young guy. He's only twenty three, and without Kevin's influence and experience it might have been a different story. He definitely brought him on. And we were thrilled to get Ja Fallon back. He was one of the best players in Galway for the past couple of years. He was a huge bonus to us when he came back. He's been a huge influence on all the young players. Course, he's good auld *craic* too, a bit of a character in the dressing-room. You wouldn't know what he would get up to next."

Adding weighty plausibility to the expectation was the management of John O'Mahony. His arrival sparked a streamlining of attitudes amongst personnel and Mac was just one player to benefit from the benchmarks O'Mahony wanted the squad to aspire to. "There was absolutely no messing with him all year. Everything was done very professionally. We were going the last couple of years thinking we could be training and having a few pints at the weekend. John stopped all that messing. It was either one or the other. A reason why we weren't having much success before was because we were kind of happy enough to be just in the side. You would play away. But John O'Mahony came in and changed our attitude this year. We knew he was a great manager, but we didn't know too much about him. Even to look at him, he would kind of frighten you really. When he sets his mind to something he means it. He's going to do his damdest to get past the finishing post."

Acknowledging O'Mahony meant business, players diligently knuckled down to their task. Preparations were time-consuming. Dedication was required in abundance. That materialised, leaving Mac to express admiration for two players, Seán Ó Domhnaill and Shay Walsh, whose unwavering efforts finally paid off. From Carraroe in the heartland of the Connemara Gaeltacht, Ó Domhnaill's commitment was consummate. That showed especially during winter training sessions at Monivea, a period when Ó Domhnaill was regularly called ashore and substituted in national league games. "It was an hour-and-a-half of a drive to Monivea and an hour-and-a-half back for him. Every training session used to take two-and-a-half hours, maybe three hours sometimes. That was some commitment to do that three times a week after doing an eight-to-five job as well. He deserved a lot of credit for doing that. Coming up to the championship he was kind of touch and go whether he would be playing or not, and he still kept going." Walsh is another to earn praise. "At the start of the year it looked like Shay hadn't got a chance of getting a game. He wasn't fit and he wasn't playing well. Everything was going wrong, but he kept going and he ended up playing in the All-Ireland final. He just stuck with it."

Another integral piece in the pie was the captaincy of Ray Silke, Mac's club colleague at Corofin. Mac himself was offered the position but the goalkeeper turned down the offer of captaincy on swift realisation that his compatriot was the prime suspect for the job. Having since witnessed Silke hoist both club and county All-Irelands, it would be no surprise if Mac was just a tad envious on reflection. Far from it. "If I was complaining about that there would be people trying to check me out. Ray Silke was the captain of our club team and he was an absolutely brilliant captain. John O'Mahony's a great man for talk before a game, but Ray is also good. When he talks everybody listens. There's no such thing as banging on tables or shouting or screaming. He just says things short and sweet, everything to the point. He was a better choice as captain, so I didn't mind passing it over to him. I'd be one of the quieter fellas and I'm happy enough. I'm content with what I have."

                    *   *   *   *

Galway's journey to the All-Ireland final was not for the faint-hearted. Emotional highs were countered by some lows which placed questions over their ability to pilfer the big prize. Biggest of all those interrogations came from Roscommon. Galway souls were comprehensively assessed following a chastening wake-up call in Tuam before positive answers emerged in the replay. Overcoming the Connacht final hurdle showed that Galway were a team eager to learn and, when absorbed, the Roscommon lessons proved critical in heralding the Tribesmen's ultimate breakthrough.

The build-up to the provincial final in Tuam had in many ways mirrored the build up to the All-Ireland final itself. For the Connacht final, Galway were hot favourites and little attention was focused on Roscommon. That role was subsequently reversed for the Croke Park final, with Galway assuming the mantle of unfancied underdogs and Kildare deemed unbackable favourites. Nevertheless, the Tuam fright had helped Galway no end, believes Martin McNamara. "We beat Mayo. It was a huge boost and then we went on to beat Leitrim fairly easily. That probably gave us too much confidence going into the Roscommon game. It was like Kildare were in the All-Ireland final, we were blown up to the last. We were red-hot favourites. We went in too easy going and we were lucky enough to get away with it and get a draw. We underestimated them. Roscommon are a good side. They're going to come good. They're going to win a Connacht final or an All-Ireland in the next couple of years if they stick together. We didn't show them the respect they should have got the first day. We did the second day and we were lucky enough again to get out of it. But things worked out right. Actually, that probably helped us to win the All-Ireland. Those two games brought us on leaps and bounds."

Mac himself excelled in the provincial final, producing some top-drawer saves. But the All-Ireland semi-final produced his most enjoyable salvo. For years Joe Brolly honed a reputation for clinical finishing and had shown against Donegal in Ulster that his scent for goal was still strong. Against Mac though, the one sniff the marksman got was smothered. "The save I get most pleasure from was Joe Brolly's shot. It just hit me in the stomach. But he'd been the danger man for Derry for the last six or seven years. I got a bit of pleasure out of that. I didn't fancy seeing him kissing the crowd. He's a nice guy, but I wouldn't have been able to take that."

*   *   *   *

The Lilywhites awaited. For all the players, it was a new situation to be in. The annual razzmatazz of Gaelic football's grandest occasion was unchartered territory but Galway's build-up was designed so that they would hit Croke Park running. A press night in Tuam helped to relieve the demands made by the media of the players. The scribes satisfied, Galway were left to get on with the business of winning the All-Ireland. One shrewd ploy was to experience the Croke Park roar on final day itself, an acclimatising exercise conducted by heading to headquarters for the All-Ireland hurling final. Mac reckons it was a keen-eyed stroke to pull. "The day of an All-Ireland final, the atmosphere is absolutely something else. We were there when the Kilkenny and Offaly teams came on to the field for the hurling final. The cheer that was there was unreal, so we kind of knew what to expect when we came out. I'd say if we didn't know what to expect our legs would have turned to jelly, but John O'Mahony left no stone unturned. When we came up we just knew what to expect and we came on to the pitch as if it was just a normal game. That helped us an awful lot as well. The first ten minutes we dominated the game. The build-up didn't bother us at all. All the pressure was on Kildare and it took them a long time to start.

"I'd be a nervous guy, so I was nervous going out in all games this year. It's always said about matches, just go and enjoy the game as much as you can. I did. I was actually talking to the umpires and joking. I found that helped me to concentrate. But the younger guys went out and they were smiling. The occasion didn't seem to bother them at all, no matter how big it was. They took it in their stride. Young guys are different now. I suppose they're better educated. I don't know if that helps or not, but they're more laidback. I couldn't believe they were so relaxed."

Not that everything ran smoothly for Galway. No matter how solid a start they had made, a period when Kildare would assume the upperhand was inevitable. It soon arrived and Galway's bright opening was quickly overshadowed to leave Mac with the dubious task of fishing the ball out of the back of his net. An unpalatable experience, Mac's cover had gone askew and Dermot Earley was presented with the simple task of palming the ball into the empty goal. Absorbing the setback was tough. And it was made tougher still for Mac as Earley bumped into him on his way back out of the small square to celebrate the score. "There was a lot of bad marking for the goal. They got in handy enough. The problem had come from further out the field. The full-back line actually did their job. They had all their guys taken up. It was a midfielder, Willie McCreery, that came through and Ray Silke had to come. Ray had to pick him up and it left Dermot Earley loose inside. It wasn't the full-back line's fault. It was a lack of communication further out really. It was hard to take, especially when Earley, as he was going out, passed and bumped into me. That made it even harder to go in and pick the ball out. Bad enough having to pick it out without having sore ribs as well."

Reaching the dressing-room at the interval, Mac was a touch worried Kildare had retired three points ahead. Dominating possession for a similar period as Galway had done earlier in the half, the Leinster champions had most scores registered. That worry though was quickly forgotten. "I was worried, but I won't admit that to too many people. In saying that, when we went in at half-time we had time to think and settle down again. I realised that the lads were all super fit. In all the games so far this year, we had dominated in the last ten minutes. The Roscommon game in Tuam was the only one we didn't dominate."

On the resumption, Galway started thunderously and Mac came into his own with some craftily executed kick-outs. Steering the ball clear from the lottery area of midfield, short kick-outs were utilised and Kevin Walsh tapped into this steady stream of possession. "The guys made it very easy on me. We had a game plan. Michael Donnellan and Seán Óg de Paor, they were playing down that line and they moved away to make a big gap for me. So all I had to do was lob it out there to Kevin. It doesn't matter what sort of a kick-out it is. As long as it is up in the air Kevin will win most of them. So I was confident putting them out and hitting them to his little patch."

Just four points separated the sides at the finish, but Galway had known from an early stage of the second half that Sam Maguire was theirs. Certain incidents cemented that inkling. Mac remembers two in particular. "I think when Seán Ó Domhnaill kicked the point and he kind of put up his hands in the air...like Seán, he's a lovely fella but he doesn't kick too many points and when I'd seen that go over I said 'geez, this is our day'. That one stands out plus Ja Fallon's sideline kick. That was probably one of the best points I've ever seen."

Tears from Mac greeted the final whistle and soon some of his Corofin colleagues, who had been on the terraces, were on hand to smother him in congratulations. An emotional crescendo for any footballer to cherish, the goalkeeper also enjoyed the spectacle that he witnessed during Galway's homecoming on the Monday evening. "Most people were behind you but you wouldn't be aware of it. It was only when we were coming home that we really noticed it. Coming over The Shannon there were people from all over Connacht there. Guys we were trying to take the ball off a couple of months ago were cheering as one. It was a great feeling."

The exuberant celebrations were of the 'once in a lifetime' nature. Thoroughly deserved they were, yet through it all Mac spares a thought for a few Galway stalwarts who had dropped off the inter-county scene only a year previously. They were players who had given dedicated service to the Galway cause, yet the one year of triumph saw them all missing. "The Galway team that was out there was the best team apart from Francis McWalter. He would have been touch and go for a corner-back position only for his work commitments. He's got his own business going. And there's a guy from Galway, Alan Mulholland. He was there for the past couple of years and he decided to pack it in this year. John Kilraine from Salthill as well, he decided not to go. He'd been with Galway for the past six-seven years as well. You have to feel sorry for these guys."

*   *   *   *

Reclining on a bar stool on a quiet Friday afternoon in his pub in Tuam, Martin McNamara is a contented man. The whirlwind generated by an All-Ireland final appearance is beginning to subside. Now it is time for reflection and for life to return to normality. Punters in the pub again openly talk football all they want. It could no longer be the distraction to Mac's preparations that it was prior to the final. Outside, the immediate knock-on tremor of having the Sam Maguire back in the county has seen Tuam's footballing credentials spruced up. Kids have lost track of their soccer and rugby diversions and instead dream excitedly of becoming central figures when the next batch of Galway footballers saunters into the game's sporting lore.

Those desiring added inspiration only need to pop along to *McNamaras* for a friendly word. Sam Maguire has already made the trek, visiting on the Wednesday following the final on the evening of the Goal challenge match against Mayo. But aside from playing host to Sam, Mac has another priceless artefact in his possession - the All-Ireland final match ball. Having had the ball in Croke Park when the final whistle went, Mac was intent to hold on to it. However, match referee John Bannon came by and said he would take it into the dressingrooms. Mac thought it was the last he had seen of it but Bannon, one of refereeing's nice guys, was on hand at the Goal match to return the ball. A great gesture for which Mac is grateful, the ball, once autographed, will be given pride of place in *McNamaras*.

Moulding a harmonious panel of players together is never easy, even at the best of times. But winning the All-Ireland is different, a special event. Lifetime friendships are forged and Galway, no matter what the future holds for the individuals who make up the squad, will be remembered forever as All-Ireland winners. "I've been with panels before but I've never known thirty guys so close in my life. They're all good guys. You wouldn't mind meeting any of them to go and have a pint with. That definitely helped us along the way. We were all one, like one big happy family."

As a parting shot from a man who constantly peppers his sentences with the genuine sentiment of 'to be honest with you', you had better believe it.

3

Helping Hands

Mick Byrne, Physiotherapist

In the modern world of sports the team off the field is just as important as the team on it. In particular, medics who possess the Midas touch, healing hands with the knack of getting players sorted and ready for action again, are much valued. The want for reliability in this sector was a responsibility John O'Mahony fully understood on taking Galway's command. Making a definitive assessment without a second thought, he enlisted the help of Mick Byrne, the Dubliner who has filled the role of physio to the Irish international soccer team for nigh on twenty years, to cope with the bruises and the knocks that could hinder Galway's precocious talents.

To people of a younger disposition the sight of Mick being involved with a G.A.A. team was something out of the ordinary, so familiar had the Irish public become to seeing the physio standing alongside Jack Charlton in soccer stadiums around the world. Who will ever forget the enthusiastic Dubliner ecstatically bear-hugging Charlton in the immediate aftermath of Ireland historic victory over England in the 1988 European Championship Finals in Germany? Likewise, the image of Mick in The Vatican in 1990 presenting an Irish jersey and football to Pope John Paul II prior to Ireland's World Cup Quarter-Final in Rome. Pitchforked into the limelight, those two scenes alone featuring Byrne become indelible memories recalled in a instant on reminiscence of the Jack Charlton years.

However, the lingering image in the public psyche of Mick being a soccer man was never further from the truth. True, he had been reared in City Quay near the Ringsend docklands, an area renowned for soccer, he coached Reds United, one of the most successful schoolboy clubs around, and he was physio for three of Dublin's more eminent teams, Shelbourne, Bohemians and Shamrock Rovers during Johnny Giles' tenure. But Mick's *grá* for Gaelic games began at an early age. Croke Park was a constant haunt every Sunday for the youngster who first played there as a ten-year-old, winning a Miller Cup with City Quay primary school. He then played football with Clann na nGael alongside Mickey Whelan, Christy Kane and Aidan Donnelly, all All-Ireland winners with Dublin, and hurling with

Fontenoy, progressing to challenge game appearances for Dublin's senior hurling and football teams.

However, he never got the nod to tog out for the big Leinster championship days. Making a debut in a challenge game at O'Toole Park against Carlow, the odd league game was the height of his inter-county football exploits and indeed, as he jokingly quips himself, his hurling career with Dublin lasted just one game - a St. Patrick's Day challenge against Antrim which saw him wind up in hospital nursing six stitches across an eye injury. Dublin glory was not to be his, but that did not deprive Mick from enjoying the big days out at Croke Park. Using his well-honed knowledge of the stadium and his Clann na nGael connections to good effect, he acted as a steward on All-Ireland final and semi-final days, a responsibility that had him showing ticket holders to their seats. It was a handy number and little did he envisage then that he would form an integral part of a medical backroom team that would capture Sam Maguire. That expertise comprised of chief physio, Aofáine Walshe, and team doctor, Jarlath Duignan.

With the great Dublin and Kerry teams ingrained in the national imagination during the seventies, interest in the game mushroomed and Mick played his part in harnessing its pulse. Getting involved with Erin's Isle, then a fledgling club based in the heart of Finglas, a sprawling city suburb in North Dublin, much time was spent actively involving the community in organised training sessions. Since then, Erin's Isle has nurtured many talents. Mick Deegan, Keith Barr and Charlie Redmond are just a trio of many well-respected players to rise to inter-county recognition, successes that have aided and abetted the assurance of the club's presence as a focal point in the community. "Erin's Isle, it's a fantastic club," explains Mick. "It's part of the community in Finglas and has done a great job for Finglas. It's been home to loads of clubs who come up at weekends and play and vice-versa, we go down to different parts of the country."

Gaelic football coursed through Mick's blood. No matter how enjoyable his involvement with Ireland was, Sunday was the day for excursions to Croke Park. A friendship was struck with John O'Mahony and led to a peripheral involvement in Leitrim's Connacht championship success in 1994 - a balmy summer for Mick considering Ireland's exploits in the American World Cup Finals. O'Mahony's elevation to the Galway post in autumn 1997 then ensured another call to arms and medical bags, an arrangement that prompted an involvement that led to heady days and All-Ireland triumph last September.

A month on from the seismic climax to an unbelievable season, Mick is still wallowing in the enormity of the occasion. An avuncular character whose personality and conversation pieces act as traits which serve to lighten the mood in any tense team camp, the year was nothing but a dream for the inner-city cub reared on jousts for the Sam Maguire and Liam McCarthy cups.

"I had been playing Gaelic football and hurling since I was eight years of age and I never played any other sport because it was my love, hurling and football. I loved it, never dreamt of playing anything else to be honest. On the streets I played soccer because it was the inner-city where I lived and most of the stuff was soccer in that area, Pearse Street, City Quay and all around. So it was soccer-orientated but I was one of a few who played Gaelic football and hurling. I'd been in Croke Park as a senior footballer with Clann na nGael. Croker had never been a stranger to me. Every year I go to all the county matches but to actually be there on All-Ireland final day with the Galway side was just a dream come true. I've got to thank John O'Mahony for that. He's a fantastic manager. He rates with any manager I've certainly been with, without a shadow of a doubt. John made all this possible for me by inviting me into the Galway set-up."

Homecomings of fêted sporting sides are nothing new to the physio. He has seen Dublin's O'Connell Street wedged tight on numerous occasions. The raucous celebrations witnessed the day after Galway won the All-Ireland are something the 56-year-old former electrician cherishes, especially as they brought back memories of trips abroad with the Irish soccer team. "It was just unreal the homecoming. I, like everyone else in the country, would sit and watch the different Gaelic teams, winning teams go back home and I would watch it on television and just look at it. But there I was on the train going to Athlone and there was a huge crowd when we arrived. And when John and Ray Silke walked across The Shannon it was absolutely lump in your throat stage. When we got to each town or village the bonfires and the sods of turf were lit like a runway going right through.

"Then all the people standing out in the rain to greet the team - it took us nine hours to get home to Galway and there was so many people it was unreal. When we got to Tuam the crowds were unbelievable. The singing of 'The Fields of Athenry' was fantastic. I've heard it on other fields, too, which were very emotional. Like, they sang it at Anfield when Ireland played Holland and the same in Belgium. And there I was actually coming into it, coming into the place, Athenry, and all the places where the actual song is about. It was fabulous. You had to savour it. You had to see it to believe you were a part of it. It was something very, very special."

On the go the whole time, Mick's brief with Galway differed somewhat from his previous arrangement with Leitrim. Living in Ashbourne, he used to drop by to Leitrim's training sessions in Meath to give the Dublin-based players a rub down and apply the strappings. It was very much an involvement on the apron of preparations. The Galway link, however, demanded the physio attend all the matches and trundle down to Tuam to ease the aches and pains endured by the players' flesh and blood challenges. Early prognosis fuelled Mick's interest. His first outing, to Drogheda for a national league fixture against Louth, triggered a passion for the game which flowed through him during the hour and left his enthusiasm thirsting for more during those formative winter months.

Injuries were Mick's prime concern but, in the public eye at least, they were few and far between. Only two really surfaced during championship matches, injuries which saw Paul Clancy substituted against Leitrim and Kevin Walsh stretchered off the second day against Roscommon. Other undisclosed injuries niggled during the campaign but Mick reveals that the whole squad of thirty were fully fit and rearing to go against Kildare in the final, a situation which he describes as unique in team sports. "We kept our injuries to ourselves during the year. But we were just lucky touch-wood that we had thirty players that went out and were great. Everything was fine. We had no injuries going into the final, which was great and I think unique as well because usually you have one or two or three injuries during the season which you'd be a bit worried about without really saying anything, you'd just keep it within the camp. We were lucky this year, to be honest."

So with the injury scene in good health, it allowed Mick to revel in the football served up by the Tribesmen. Burning up the calories with animated movements, his exuberance was such that during the All-Ireland final the *R.T.É.* cameras, at one particular moment, focused on the sideline and there was Mick, on his toes and practically on the field of play, issuing throaty instructions to the players who were no longer rationing their scoring outlay.

"We had a fantastic side. The amount of people who didn't realise, certainly Kildare didn't realise the team we had. If you'd been watching us from our league performances right up to the championship I'm sure you'd have known that here was a team ready to explode. I mean, we'd something like seventy wides in our games against Offaly in the league quarter-final, Mayo and the two games against Roscommon. You have to keep looking at this and say 'these forwards are going to click some day'. And lucky enough we just clicked in the second half. We blew Kildare away, I think. It was a brilliant game. I don't think there was a better game of football in the last ten to fifteen years in Croke Park."

Life is undeniably good following an All-Ireland success. Within a week, Mick linked up with the Irish international team for a European

Championship qualifying match against Malta. Aside from the usual banter and ribbing that is the norm on such occasions, Mick was the recipient of much congratulations from players who had seen the match. Indeed, one Galway fan was Roy Keane. He had watched the match with his parents in Manchester and had a £100 bet on Galway to take the honours. Interest was palpable within the international camp and Mick himself, given the genteel persona he paints, was seen wearing a Galway hat when Ireland played Malta at Lansdowne Road.

That was a gesture designed to give a boost to John O'Mahony's father-in-law, Mattie Towey, who had been sick in bed at the time. In a way, the magnanimous gesture illustrates the gentleman that is Mick Byrne. Forever armed with kind words and a little joke to share, his presence in the Galway camp had proven another ingredient in the All-Ireland recipe. His infinite charm obvious to all, the tale of Patrick's Day 1998 is emblematic of his character. Even though his Erin's Isle club, by a strange quirk of irony, were defeated by Corofin in the All-Ireland club championship final, Mick steadfastly remained his noble-self. He did not even get to Croke Park that afternoon because, true to the Galway cause, he nursed the knocks during a challenge game that morning against Kildare in Celbridge. Opting to watch the club game on television rather than rush into the city, he was "bitterly disappointed" for Erin's but thrilled for the Corofin players who were involved in the Galway set-up.

A kindred spirit, Mick Byrne's place in the whole scheme of 1998's success is yet another plus in a year of many great additions to Galway football.

*   *   *   *

Stephen Joyce, Selector

Such was the freshness inherent in Galway 1998 that personnel links with previous All-Ireland final teams were conspicuous by their absence. Just one old comrade from another sojourn was on board and he came intent on exorcising the ghost of 1983. A game that went down in footballing folklore for all the wrong reasons, fourteen-man Galway failed to overcome twelve-man Dublin in one of the most controversial finals in recent decades.

It was a setback that flustered Stephen Joyce, one of the more exquisite forwards of that era. Blessed with grit and artistry, his repertoire of silky skills deserved more. Instead, folly - most vivid when Barney Rock's forty metre lob went over the stranded keeper Pauric Coyne and into the gaping net - felled Galway. It left Stephen, one of the West's most revered stalwarts, without the ultimate medal in his possession, a glaring exception in an inter-county career that stretched from 1976 to 1989. The defeat, infamous for the burst of petulance that brought sending-offs for Galway's Tomás Tierney and Dublin's Brian Mullins, Ray Hazley and Ciarán Duff, left a bittersweet aftertaste.

Without reservation, that raw September Sunday earmarked a nemesis in his playing career. And worse, the disappointment of being turned over by Dublin was further crystallised just a week later when, playing for his club Clonbur, Stephen was defeated in the only senior county final he ever got to play in. "They were huge disappointments for me, both of them. The only senior county final I'd played in and the only All-Ireland senior final I'd played in and I'd lost both of them in the one week. It was a terrible bad day the day of the All-Ireland. The fact that we were playing Dublin meant there was huge hype surrounding the game. Dublin were the team that brought hype into the game, themselves and Kerry. It was huge and we got caught up in it. We weren't prepared for it and the game kind of passed us by. There were the sendings-off and all the incidents. We ended up having the extra players but we didn't plan for it. Nowadays, you try and cover every angle. If a player is sent off, you've already made plans for who's going to be the extra man."

The doomsayers, the national media, blamed Galway's inability to deliver the 1983 All-Ireland as one of the primary reasons for a perceived decline in later years. It portrayed a requiem fall-out from that game and the fact that Galway were within twenty seconds of another final appearance in 1987, before a late Cork point denied them, was never given any credence. Assumptions lingered and that, added to the rise of the Galway hurlers, saw support for the footballers dramatically eroded. So minute did the Western support become, Galway's subsequent All-Ireland semi-finals in Croke Park never captured public attention. Unfair when you consider that Stephen won five Connacht championship medals and one national league medal during the decade.

"In the media there was an awful lot of hype based around 1983, that it was the death of Galway football. But it was unfair to say that we were finished. We had won the league in '81 and won the Connacht championship again in '84, '86 and '87, so we were continually there or thereabouts. Against Cork in '87, we had gone the extra point up and time was practically up. But they drew and beat us well in the replay. Yet when we got to All-Ireland semi-finals, there wouldn't have been two thousand Galway people in Croke Park to support us. That was disappointing. We would be running out on Croke Park and there was hardly a cheer. It was unfair then the way '83 did affect us."

Not that Stephen, a 41-year-old Telecom employee, looks back in anger. The disappointments do not frame his playing career but as a selector they were not forgotten. Having learned the quicksilver quality of knowing how to motivate players, the build-up to the All-Ireland final was garnished with the importance that the Galway players accept their chance to win it. Stephen was the perfect candidate for the hard luck story as five All-Ireland semi-finals produced only one final spot in which honours went Dublin's way. He believed at the time that more final appearances would arise but they never happened, thus giving Stephen the added incentive to impress upon the current crop in maroon jerseys that they might only ever get one chance and should devote everything to maximising it.

"When I played in the final in '83, I thought I would be back to play in another final but I wasn't. I think whatever age you are, whether you're nineteen, twenty, twenty six or thirty, when you get one chance you have to take it - the opportunity may never come again. You may get hurt, you may lose form, you can never depend on 'well, there'll always be next year'. You have to take the opportunity when it's there and we tried to get it across to them and obviously it worked. When I was playing I did genuinely feel at the time that we would be back in an All-Ireland final again. It didn't happen. We got within twenty seconds of it but we didn't get there." Emphasis on accepting this opportunity of a lifetime in a lifetime of opportunity helped generate a positive attitude in the build-up to this year's final. Galway just thought of winning.

Prior to jumping on board the O'Mahony All-Ireland express, Stephen's only prior involvement at inter-county management level was helping out with training the 1989 Galway minor team. That prologue gave a brief insight to the requirements of life on the preparation side. And having been involved for so long as a player he was aware of the commitment necessary and that commitment, compared to his own days, now requires even more of an effort. There would be nothing passive about the job. Proving susceptible to its allure after giving the offer from O'Mahony due consideration, he felt he would be able to meet the intensity and fill the role. Happy to get involved in the dynamic flux, he took the first tentative steps in September 1997.

"I knew obviously from having played myself that there was huge commitment and I knew that it was probably even more so now because the thing has gone more professional. I knew that if I was going to be involved I had to be able to give it the full whack. Definitely we were better prepared this time for an All-Ireland. We were focused on the job in hand. We had thirty players on the panel and the commitment given this year all-round by that panel was great. When I was playing myself I always gave one hundred per cent, but I think it would have been more accepted then that a fella missed training for one reason or another - it was easier. It couldn't be accepted now. The level of fitness, the level of what's needed to win an All-Ireland now takes total commitment."

With Peter Warren given special detail to monitor the defence and former Galway player, Gay McManus, training the Dublin-based players, Stephen was given dispatch to take the forwards under his wing and utilise his knowledge in that sector. Recognising the sparkling quality present though, it was a brief he approached with a dose of realism. As he says himself: "You don't teach a fella like Ja Fallon how to play football. The thing we had to try to do was to co-ordinate the whole thing and try to get the best type of game from them. If a team wins you're great on the sideline and if you don't - well, you know yourself. We had a certain game plan that we tried to put into operation and it worked."

An intrinsic ingredient in Galway's eminence in 1998 was the settled nature of their team. So settled was it that when Paul Clancy came on as a substitute in the All-Ireland final it meant they finished the championship season with the same team that started it the previous May against Mayo in Castlebar. That signalled a boundless familiarity percolating within the camp and that proved crucial. Another plus for the managerial newcomers was the regal bond the younger players in the squad had from their days of playing together in other grades.

"A lot of them would have played college, they would have played minor and they would have played U-21s, so they knew each others play. I think that with the experienced players in along with them, the whole thing gelled together and we had some combination. The young fellas having played together wouldn't have won anything without the Ja Fallons or the Seán de Paors to help them settle. The whole thing came together for us and we brought the younger fellas on with the older fellas and it worked out."

Going well in the league, the prospect of an earlier than envisaged Croke Park outing dawned when Galway faced Offaly in a national league quarter-final at Dr. Hyde Park. They lost but, in hindsight, the missed opportunity of not getting a centre-stage rehearsal was not a hindrance. "The main focus was one game at a time but at the same time you had to look ahead. When we played Offaly in the quarter-final, we wanted to win it because we felt that the game in Croke Park would be a huge benefit to us, especially if we were to get back there again later on in the year.

"But the big obstacle, of course, was the first round of the championship and once we got over that we felt we were in with a great chance. We ourselves thought we might have won the Offaly game and we expected to win it, but certainly it wasn't the end of the world that we didn't win it. It probably was the best thing that ever happened to us. Once the Offaly game was over we regrouped and put the focus into the championship. Training was all geared towards the May 24th in Mayo. There was nothing else, just May 24th. That was our All-Ireland Final. If we didn't get over that that was the end of the line."

The history books now show that Mayo, ironically the county with whom Stephen, a pupil at Ballinrobe Vocational School, won an All-Ireland Vocational Schools medal with in 1975, were not the calibre they had been the previous two years. From there, the inkling that something special was about to happen fermented, yet Galway made their way into an All-Ireland final to find Kildare embossed as the untouchables. The fact that Galway were not rated in the chic capital paid a disservice to Connacht football but at the same time, it allowed them hone their tactics without much intrusion. "I don't think the hype of being thirty two years without an All-Ireland put any pressure on us this year. We decided we would take a low-key approach to it. Kildare were made red-hot favourites and that suited us grand.

"The thirty two years was irrelevant. We were concentrating on 1998 and what happened before that or after that wasn't going to make any difference to us. We were just concentrating on 1998. We always believed we had the team good enough to do it. We would obviously look at the opposition but it was not about what they can do. We'd a better team and it was what we could do on the day. We felt that Croke Park was no different to any other pitch. If we played to our full potential, we were going to win the match regardless of what the opposition was going to do, be it Derry or

Kildare. We knew on both occasions they were made hot favourites and there was nothing drawing attention on us. But we knew that if we could put our game plan across and play to our potential, we were going to beat either of them."

The win was secured with a sweep and rhythm that rekindled talk of yesteryear and the sixties. It even has Stephen delving back into childhood memories of 1966, the year Galway were last acquainted with the Sam Maguire. Back then, as a youngster growing up in Clonbur, Mattie McDonagh's winning goal against Meath was often recreated by Stephen and friends in back gardens. It was a spur that helped him play U-16 football at the age of thirteen and spawned an ambition to represent Galway.

"I remember the last of the three-in-a-row. That would be the big thing in my mind. I don't remember the others because I would have been only nine. I just remember watching the '66 match in somebody else's house because we didn't have a telly at the time. Mattie McDonagh scored the goal but I don't remember an awful lot more about it. You'd then be playing football in the fields afterwards and you'd be imagining you'd be Seamus Leydon or Mattie McDonagh."

Now a new generation of Galway children have fresh heroes to idolise. With images of 1998 acting as a positive catalyst, Stephen anticipates a huge surge of interest in the game in the region. "It's hugely important. The hype in Galway since the All-Ireland has been unreal. It will bring football on no end in Galway. We'll have all the kids out wanting to play for their county and not maybe Man Utd or Liverpool or any other cross-channel teams. It will have a huge impact on football, possibly in the West as well as Galway."

No doubt it will. But, in the meantime, Galway football can reflect on the aesthetic of the occasion, happy that Stephen Joyce, one of their most dedicated performer a decade ago, now has that elusive All-Ireland medal in his possession. Just goes to show nice guys do come first in sport.

*   *   *   *

Pete Warren, Selector

Intensity surrounds Gaelic in Tuam. The town's deep commitment to the sport is one of the most vibrant features of the game in Connacht. A hotbed where colleges and clubs collide in kaleidoscopic fashion, rivalries evolved from decades ago produces many stalwarts with an endless enthusiasm to add their scripture to the game's growing gospel.

Time-consuming that commitment to football may be, it is one Pete Warren would not swap for anything. Weaned in St. Patrick's College, Tuam, his interest flourished at Tuam Stars where, while still a player, he became the first to manage the illustrious club to a Connacht club championship in 1994. Previous to that, back-to-back county titles in 1988 and 1989 led to his involvement with the Galway senior side which he captained for a national league campaign. But it marked the biggest splash in Pete's shortlived inter-county career. Injured for the 1990 Connacht final which Galway lost, Pete, not scaling the commanding heights in the maroon jersey, was never to win a provincial title. Not having played for the Tribesmen in Croke Park, Pete was convinced the cherished moment of being involved with a team at headquarters had long since passed.

However, things change quickly in the ever-changing forum that is modern day inter-county football. On a recommendation, John O'Mahony sought his involvement in autumn 1997 and the dye was cast. A selector with a special accord to monitor defensive play, the niche position brought unheralded All-Ireland riches. Instant success is beyond the realm of fantasy. Galway football examined its conscience and emerged re-energised at the other end of the spectrum with the Sam Maguire in its possession. Nothing could put the mockers on the audacious achievement.

"For me not to reach the heights as a player ,to get into Croke Park and be involved in an All-Ireland final as a selector was as good to me now as it was playing. To win an All-Ireland final, it's the highest feat for anyone. It's the highest mark any player, any selector, any manager can achieve. To get it is a fantastic achievement and we have done it and done it in one year. Most people would say that when you reach that goal that'll be it but when you reach it and you're over it like we are, then you're saying to yourself 'are we going to go for another one?'. It was a high, it was a great feeling and we were very lucky to be in the situation to have won it at this stage." Not bad for a man who celebrated his forty second birthday on the Saturday before the All-Ireland final.

Winning the All-Ireland marks a breakthrough for Connacht following decades of scant reward at inter-county level. But talismanic breakthroughs are nothing new to Pete. For twenty three years, Tuam Stars, an illustrious club steeped in the history of winning county titles, were left to endure a lack of success. Altering the etiquette established when Tuam Stars, possessing the impeccable talents of Sean Purcell and Frank Stockwell, dominated, other clubs flourished in creating a new order. Only in 1984 did Tuam Stars bounce back amongst the big-hitters. It was a timely breakthrough and Pete was to end his playing days with four county titles to his credit, a harvest not foreseen at the beginning of the eighties. Tuam's eventual successful repeal of the new order served to exemplify the reverence for the game in North Galway. But it was tough going. There was nothing stuffy and dull in that neck of the woods.

"Tuam is the centre of football and Tuam Stars have been, I suppose, the most noted club in the county going back years and years ago, even to Sean Purcell's and Frank Stockwell's time. Clubs like Corofin, Mountbellew, Killererin and Dunmore, they're all on the outskirts within a radius of not more than ten miles. All the football is in that area and all the lads from the clubs are coming and going. They all went to school with each other and they would meet each other in town. We had fifty thousand here on the Monday night of the All-Ireland final. I've been playing with Tuam and I was manager of Tuam and even when we won our first Connacht final the crowds were around but we never realised there was that many people in the area. Everyone knows everyone, it's grand. There's a bit of rivalry between clubs and all that but that's good. Like, that's in the game. Let it bring some good."

Another melting pot factor that makes Tuam the thriving footballing hotbed is St. Jarlaths College. The alumni, source of so many talented footballers, not only for Galway but for other Connacht counties also, is forever contributing handsomely to the make-up of Galway inter-county sides. In technical terms it is a production line, one that nurtures a quality supply which provides an abundance of choice and continuity for selectors of Tribesmen teams. In 1998 alone, thirteen of the Galway panel hailed from Jarlaths and many of them were the fruits of the 1994 Hogan Cup winning team. The biggest school in the area, Jarlaths has the pick of the youngsters, an envious position that generates much competition from other schools on the football fields. A product of St. Patrick's College, one of Jarlaths' main adversaries, Pete knows all about that rivalry.

"The difference we saw when we played them was they had the pick. They had a huge pick and I suppose that's why they were successful. In my first year I happened to be on the first juvenile team to beat Jarlaths in 1969 or 1970 after so many years and that was a great thing for us. Football is a tradition in Jarlath's. The colleges' competition is a huge thing and they've been in many a final. Teams following on have to keep up with the previous stars and, I suppose, that's the reason they produce the players."

Aside from Pete, embellishing the role Tuam played in Galway's All-Ireland success is the presence of one of their own, Jarlath Fallon. Lost to rugby in September 1997 and with a potential professional contract in the offing, a return to football for Ja was not on the horizon. But it did not require a genius to spot his imperious worth. Enticing the ball-juggling maestro back in the county colours would iron out one of the last kinks absent from the All-Ireland chasing inventory. As the rugby season lurched into its dying embers last April, a plan to solve the conundrum was hatched. The player's counsel was sought and the riposte was a real fillip.

"Ja had been into the rugby and he was hoping to get a contract. We felt it very important that Ja would be in the set-up because he is a fantastic player and you need him, you definitely need him. At first, we had a problem getting him back because he was so into the rugby. Then towards the end of the season, John, myself and Stephen Joyce sat and we spoke about how we were going to get Ja back. I rang him and asked could we meet him, so Stephen and myself went to his house and we told him the situation.

"He is a very modest, quiet lad and he didn't know how the players would react to him coming in after missing the league. But the camaraderie in the panel was great because when Ja came in the first night of a meeting, the first reaction from one of the panel was a big round of applause for him. So he automatically settled in straightaway. And that goes to show the panel that we have. It was great. They were only delighted to see him coming back. There was none of this thing that he was missing for the last few months. They were just delighted to see him back because they knew Ja as well as anyone else. And that's why there was a great panel there. They just wanted to win, no matter who was going to be on the team."

That cameo alone indicates much about the unbreakable team spirit within the Galway ranks. Soundbites from both Ray Silke and O'Mahony throughout the year added to the harmony. The party line was that this was never just about the fifteen players who took the field on any one occasion. It was about the twenty four who stripped for every game and the six who completed the training panel of thirty. All eager to play, the man-management ensured they stuck together in a 'one for all, all for one' strategy. One character who expounded the inclusive theme is Pete.

"No-one was ever left out. We'd have the job of picking the team and we picked the subs and unfortunately there were six players who didn't make the twenty four and John had the task of telling those players. It was not an easy job to tell six guys they hadn't made the panel, but there was always the next game. The lads took it well. John rang them or talked to them personally and explained to them the decision. We all tried to get them as close to the sideline with the team as possible so they'd all be together. Then when the game was over we'd all meet and have the bit of *craic*. And they were all fighting to get in for the next game and so on. We always held on to the thirty, and even though there were six lads who didn't make the All-Ireland final panel they were still delighted to be there."

Open communication was priceless and it helped hone the footballing style that won the All-Ireland with panache, rejuvenating memories of an ageing era. Pete, then an impressionable ten-year-old, was at the 1966 final, a triumph that marked the finale of Galway's three-in-a-row. That day out allows him to understand why the style of the modern day team is being mirrored with teams of old.

"One thing older people have said about this All-Ireland, the second half in particular, is that it reminded them of back in the sixties - '64, '65, '66 - when Galway would have got the ball and they would have kicked a long ball into the forward line, then taken one or two passes and put the ball over the bar. This was the older generation saying it was a fantastic second half, that it was typical of the way we played in the sixties."

But Galway's breakthrough in 1998 is not just a celebration within the county boundary. It transcends the province, a unifying denominator which Pete, through his travels as a sales rep throughout Counties Galway, Mayo and Roscommon, fully recognises. Football is the common language in other counties, serving as a supporting cast to back Galway. It is a unity rarely seen in other provinces where local rivalries fester and never forgotten. "Mayo, in the last two years, were very unlucky not to win an All-Ireland and I never felt more sorry. Everyone in Galway and Roscommon and everywhere else followed Mayo in their All-Irelands and they were unlucky that they didn't win one. The same support happened with Galway. I remember meeting two men in the Burlington after Croke Park on the Sunday night. They were two Mayo men with two Galway jerseys on them. They had said that when Galway beat Mayo in Castlebar they automatically said they were going to follow whoever comes out of Connacht. They didn't necessarily say Galway, they said whoever comes out of Connacht they'd be following. And it was us.

"I've met Roscommon men and they have been up in Tuam, they've been up in Galway, and they followed us down from Athlone. It has been incredible the amount of people from other counties that have followed

Galway. Indeed for the homecoming that was part of the reason why we had fifty thousand people in Tuam. We had people from Sligo, Leitrim, Mayo, Roscommon all here on the Monday night and it was great. People just wanted the Sam Maguire to come across The Shannon after thirty two years. It was incredible. You were automatically the talking point of the whole country. Everything was about Galway, Galway football and anytime a conversation came up about Galway, football always came into it. It was amazing really." Amazing indeed, particularly as Pete is a big fan of the Kerry side during the seventies. Back then, Mike Sheehy, Eoin 'Bomber' Liston and John Egan annually chased All-Irelands and followed in the evolution of Pete's boyhood respect for Jimmy Duggan, Liam Sammon and Johnny Geraghty, his favourites from the 1966 All-Ireland winning outfit.

Now Galway has new idols and Pete, through his involvement as a selector, is one of them. He now predicts a dramatic rise in the game's fortunes within the county. "The whole thing about us winning the All-Ireland is that it will be a huge turnaround for Galway football. Everywhere you go now around the country and town areas, lads are out playing football. These lads haven't played football before but they are now into it. They have all got the Tommy Varden jersies. It is probably the best thing to ever happen to Galway football. You've got the Sam Maguire and you're bringing it into the schools. It has converted lads."

A season of untold riches concluded, expect Pete to be back in an attempt to cement that conversion further in 1999.

4

The Golden Years

Sean Purcell, The Formidable Fifties

Every sporting domain has its grandmasters, individuals whose legend in the sporting firmament has been enshrined and still continues to be the glittering benchmark for others to aspire to. Gaelic football in Galway is no different. Its heroes of yesteryear, a period drama that dazzled with Connacht titles and All-Irelands galore, are fondly revered. Occupying positions of reverence never to be impeached, Mattie McDonagh, Enda Colleran and Frankie Stockwell are just a trio of the more prominent starlets to have worn the maroon jersey with gusto. But one player's deeds truly deserving of consummate plaudits is Sean Purcell. A college star with St. Jarlaths in 1946 and 1947 when they lost and won All-Ireland colleges finals, Sean, known by definition as 'The Master', became a permanent fixture in the Galway side for well over a decade. One All-Ireland medal, in 1956, coronated an inter-county career enriched by six provincial titles, five of them in a row between 1956 and 1960, and a national league medal in 1957.

He further captained the unsuccessful Galway side in the 1959 All-Ireland decider, a game where he lined out at full-forward. But that position was only a temporary home. Such was Sean's incredible versatility, he previously played at full-back, centre-back, midfield and centre-forward - every one a central position that required equal vigour and a tutored eye. Adding to his renown, he captained Connacht to Railway Cup success in 1958, his third win in that competition, and his aptitude for the sport was crowned with the winning of seven county titles in a row with his Tuam Stars club. A mover and a shaker, his honoured contours are still of such importance that in the 1998 All-Ireland final programme a full page is devoted to the quietly-spoken 'Master'. Decades on from his heyday, the limelight is still his. And rightly so.

Although now a sprightly 69-year-old, his newsagent premises in Tuam remains a haunt constantly frequented by all desiring a wise word on the sport he cherishes. There, Gaelic football magazines lie prominently on the counter. And one portraying a cover shot of Seán Óg de Paor, one of Galway's class of '98, wearing an Ireland jersey is particularly apt.

Four weeks on from the positive reverberations of Sam Maguire's homecoming, football chat still courses through every sinew of the game's North Galway capital. Sean himself is taken aback by it all, particularly the buzz that enraptured the town. "It's great for the young people, they're really gone wild over this team and it augurs well for the future of the county. The homecoming was amazing. I never saw such a crowd in Tuam, all the kids..." As someone surrounded by footballing greatness in his prime, he is equally thrilled that Sam Maguire's thirty two year sabbatical away from the province is at an end. "It really was a wonderful thing, a wonderful feeling to win after thirty two years. It was a wonderful thing for Connacht football, which has been knocked quite a bit over the years. It was looked upon as the ugly duckling but now that has changed all round. It helped to do a great deal for the image of the game. I think it will be remembered as one of the great finals. It was a great, emotional occasion. It was one of the finest games I've seen in that it was a very clean game with no unseemly incidents at all in it and I think it will give a great uplift to the game in the West and generally all over. It was a great thing for Galway football, too, that this year Corofin won the All-Ireland club championship. It was the beginning of a really great year for Galway."

What pleases 'The Master' most on watching events unfold from his position of eminence is that the All-Ireland victory is just reward for the crafted efforts of both management and players. "We had a great panel and a very good management team. O'Mahony was a great trainer. He made a great input to this team. He's a very good manager, the best in the game now and he certainly got on well with the lads and got the best out of them. That was the approach he had, he left nothing to chance. Apart from John O'Mahony, the two helpers, Peter Warren here in Tuam who was a great clubman for Tuam in his day and Stephen Joyce who still plays club football and was really an outstanding player in his own right, had an input into this team as well." But victories are mostly about the players, however. Without reservation, Sean is glowing in his praise. Those, in particular, to receive the seal of approval from 'The Master' are Michael Donnellan and Tuam's own Jarlath Fallon. "The signs have been good over the last few years and the final in September was the climax. The last four years, since '95 when we were beaten by Tyrone in the semi-final, have been promising. About half of that team was still there from that semi-final and in that time if we had Tomás Mannion and Jarlath Fallon fit we could certainly have won the '95 one and we would have been there or thereabouts since. But with those two lads fit and available and a great crop of young footballers, like Michael Donnellan, the Joyces, young Savage and Divilly, the underage players you might say, coming through - they made a big impact and I think they will be there for a while yet.

"Michael Donnellan's a tremendous footballer. I saw him playing in the colleges final for Jarlaths a few years ago and he was really outstanding. And, of course, he was outstanding in the final this year. There's no limit to where he can go. He's really an outstanding athlete. He has a great burst of speed, together with all the other skills. He's something else." Then there is Jarlath Fallon. "I must say that at half-time in the All-Ireland final I was just a little worried. But I knew Jarlath hadn't opened up yet, and when he did as he had done in all the other games this year in the second half he really turned on the style and gave a great display. It was great to be watching it. It was a wonderful game of football. I'm delighted for the lads, all the lads. They put an awful lot of work in and they deserved success."

The All-Ireland triumph for the province was long in coming. Sam Maguire's absence had rendered Connacht football the poor relation of the four provincial cousins and displays by its teams in Croke Park were often only paid compliments through gritted teeth. That attitude distorted the reality that Connacht did have a competitive edge, especially in recent years, comparable to other provinces. Now, the winning of an All-Ireland should alter the perception of others and openly earn the game deserved praise from other quarters. Sean, for one, believes Connacht, and especially Galway football, is up there on the podium as a marker for others to copy. "In the last few years there has been some very good games in Connacht. Mayo were certainly unlucky not to win at least one of the two All-Irelands finals. They were quite capable of winning, but the ball didn't hop for them. And I had been hopeful for the last few years that Galway would make the final breakthrough. There's no reason why they shouldn't go on. If they can stay together they must have a great chance. They're a very young team, they have a great panel and there will be many more footballers coming along. It's hard to know from season to season, from year to year, who is going to keep going. The commitment to football now is tremendous and it is very hard to expect the work to be put in every year. We should get over London anyway next May, but you can't take anything for granted now. Every county is geared up for the championship from the beginning of the year."

Gearing up for the championship in the old days, Sean's former playing colleagues used to enjoy welcoming him back into the fold whenever he would have been absent. The story goes, according to present goalkeeper Martin McNamara, that when 'The Master' took a break for a while, be it through injury or otherwise, he always arrived back at training a couple of weeks before the championship. Delighted with his return and the realisation that it boosted the prospect of success that season, the players would always meet Sean at the gate. He would have the plastic bag with the boots in it and the players always clapped him in.

Not that such reverence was reserved for Sean alone. He had a brother in charm, Frankie Stockwell, and together, following a description given to them by G.A.A. broadcaster and writer Mick Dunne, they were to become know as the 'Terrible Twins'. His great friend had returned to Galway following a brief flirtation in the Louth colours and when the moment of reckoning arrived in the 1956 All-Ireland, Frankie, destined for great things, demolished Cork's hopes with 2-5 from play - a scoring record in a final that has remained unequalled ever since. "We've been buddies all our lives. There was a good combination there all right between us. Frankie's record in that game, 2-5 from play in a sixty minute final and he had a goal disallowed, will never be equalled. That was Frank's day, there's no doubt at all about that. But on any occasion he could play on his own. He was a wonderful athlete. Even though he wasn't very big physically, he had a great spring."

Just as Galway's 1998 All-Ireland marks a revival of the footballing classics and the return of the Tribesmen to the top of the pile, provincial triumph in 1954 was a similar rising following a lengthy spell wallowing in the depths of mediocrity. A first Connacht title since 1945, it spawned the catalyst that flowered into an All-Ireland win in 1956. For Sean, it capped a great period where football was the staple diet of the population's social outings. Sunday was the big day out, a tradition handed down to the modern era.

"The one that always comes to mind is the '54 semi-final against Mayo down here in Tuam when we had a great comeback. We beat Mayo that day and we made the breakthrough that we needed to go on and win the 1956 All-Ireland. In '56. it was eighteen years since Galway had won the All-Ireland in '38. There was always a great football tradition in Galway, especially in North Galway. Mayo and Roscommon had good teams in between, especially Roscommon during the war years. There was always great interest in football. It was nearly the main interest of people at that time. They hadn't as many distractions as they have today. People grew up and played the game, so there was always great interest in it. I remember going to one of the Roscommon finals in the early forties on the train and when you think there used to be up to seventy, eighty thousand people at these games during the war years, it was wonderful."

It also helped that football within the locality was strong, with Sean's own Tuam Stars the measure for others to match. "It was a wonderful time to be young and playing football. We had a good team, a great team here in Tuam. We had great times. They were a great bunch of lads, great memories. Tuam was almost always there to be shot at and all the neighbouring clubs had their own footballing traditions."

But there were differences between winning All-Irelands then and what is required now. The most obvious fingered by Sean is fitness, though Galway would have taken the same approach then to the big matches by making the trip to Dublin on the Saturday prior to playing on the Sunday. "We would have stayed overnight. But, I suppose, it was not the same kind of preparation they do now. Players have to do harder preparation now. It seems to last all year, a long build-up. The fitness level of the players is the most remarkable thing. I'd say in the fifties you trained for a few weeks and you'd gradually build-up over the summer. You'd be playing a bit of football all along, but we weren't training as much as they do now. That would be the size of it. There was a welcome home in '56. Not as grand a scale as it was this year, but it was a joyful occasion, too."

The curtain on Sean's illustrious inter-county career came down during a bizarre Connacht final day in Castlebar in 1962. Remembered memorably as the joust during which the crossbar came crashing down following the efforts of Roscommon goalkeeper, Aidan Brady, to prevent a score, Galway were pipped by a point when play finally resumed. It was the second year in a row Roscommon had got the better of them. Not that Sean minded too much. His great opponent, Gerry O'Malley, finally had something tangible to show for his years of marking Sean. "I had a good run at it. Gerry O'Malley was a great opponent of mine, a great footballer and a great gentleman. I used to meet him quite often at matches. He never lost his good humour. He looks as young as ever, a really great footballer, a sporting footballer."

Although Sean's active involvement in the sport has gradually receded over the decades, he remains an avid spectator, attending all Galway and Tuam Stars matches under the guise of his role as the current president of the Galway Football Board. "That's a very honorary position. I'd look at it that way. It's a great honour to be there obviously, especially the year when Galway won the All-Ireland. It doesn't entail great work on my part though." But, in truth, it does. Modest to the last, 'The Master', a luminary of days long ago whose star still shines brightly.

*   *   *   *

Mattie McDonagh, The Swinging Sixties

Unbridled excitement swept throughout County Galway when the Sam Maguire was finally won after a thirty two year hiatus. Natives revelled in the jubilant atmosphere the thunderous triumph brokered. The victory transcended everyone and celebrations of the remarkable upsurge of footballing fortunes are only to be expected. Nevertheless, a sense of irony attaches the phrases that wax lyrical about the Galway crew of 1998. Descriptive words choicely illustrate the virtues of the players who have just won their first All-Ireland medals. They are richly deserved but it makes one wonder what words had accompanied the fanfare for Mattie McDonagh, the Galway gladiator who won a fourth All-Ireland medal in 1966. An unprecedented haul, it remains unequalled in the West of Ireland, an area of the country where the All-Ireland has been won just thirteen times.

Mattie was a player of great accomplishment, a footballing icon and a feisty competitor who encapsulated the grandeur of the game during that fascinating era. Central to Galway's trilogy of All-Ireland successes in the sixties, Mattie, as a precocious 18-year-old, also raised eyebrows with his youthful showing when the Tribesmen took the 1956 All-Ireland. A player whose motto for life was to win with integrity, his success-laden career pushed back the conventional boundaries that normally restricted the amount of honours won by footballers in Connacht.

Four All-Ireland medals were backboned by a colossal collection of ten Connacht titles, a 1958 Railway Cup and two national league successes - glittering reward for a player equipped with an extraordinary toughness of spirit to match the commitment required to play amongst the elite for over a decade. And his versatility was such that he was also a dab hand at hurling, winning a Roscommon senior county medal for Ballygar in 1952 at the sombre age of fourteen. Possessing a unique flair, he weaved a tapestry that saw him honoured as the *Texaco* Gaelic Footballer of the Year for 1966, the occasion when his goal proved decisive against Meath in the All-Ireland final. A fêted local, the honour was deserved national recognition for his achievements in the days before the All-Star awards gave players their due.

Unquestionably, life was good back then. The swinging sixties saw Ireland rocking. Being peerless in one's chosen sport added to the aura of the era. But Mattie, now the 61-year-old principal of Creggs National School in County Roscommon, contrasts certain similarities between then and now. A man of searing honesty who still cuts a remarkable figure, he believes, on witnessing All-Ireland 1998, that it is a firm indicator that the good times are coming around again, just as they had done in his heyday. "I have compared the sixties to the current era and Ireland is booming at the moment. Ireland was booming in the sixties. People were coming back in the sixties to settle here. It was a time when there was great music and showbands. There was a life in the country that time that was incomparable to anything that went before it and the same thing is happening again. You have the economy going strong, you have football going well. People have money to spend, they have cars to get around. And there's great excitement because of the win."

And Mattie is just as excited as everyone else. As a player or manager, the celebrations and general enjoyment of an All-Ireland final weekend naturally differs from the exuberant *bonhomie* that spectators revel in. Going to Croke Park for the game against Kildare last September, Mattie was in the unusual position of having no active involvement with the team. But far from diluting his enthusiasm for the fray, it offered a refreshing perspective that added to the whole occasion. "As somebody said to me lately, they were enjoying football more now they weren't involved in it. We went to the K Club in Straffan on the Saturday and played golf. That was a great start to the day and then we went on the Pat Kenny show and then to a football club in Dublin where we were presented with statuettes for the three-in-a-row. The next day there was the match, then the getting ready and going out to the function in The Burlington. There was nothing like the whole day or the whole weekend, it was fabulous.

"When you're playing football you're very restricted. I remember we were playing Down on one occasion and you could see all the Down fans going down to Croke Park and we were kind of resting in the hotel. You were saying 'they had more fun than the actual players' because you were minding yourself for weeks. You had trained hard and you couldn't just go out on the town and enjoy yourself, though you could afterwards. You wouldn't exchange it naturally, but there was a lot to be said for the freedom of just watching and enjoying it."

That value of being on the other side was further embellished when Galway trundled homewards with the Sam Maguire to be toasted at every crossroads. "I was with the team on part of the journey around Mountbellew and it was chaotic. There was great excitement and it reminded me very much of the same happening in the three-in-a-row. But the fact that it was a thirty two year of a gap, there was probably more excitement this time then I've ever noticed before. And I could enjoy it as an onlooker rather than being involved. I used to find that up on a lorry you were being paraded. I didn't particularly like it. You felt a little bit like somebody in the zoo being looked at. And I didn't appreciate the value of it to the young people at the time. It was only when I was with the Galway team in '86 that won the All-Ireland minor title - I was a selector with John Tobin - and we brought the cup into Ballygar that I realised what it meant to the young people. We had Tomás Kilcommins and Padraic Fallon of the Ballygar team on it and they had a torchlight procession with bonfires and speeches from the bridge just on the Roscommon border to Ballygar."

Mattie enjoyed the social side of the occasion in 1998 more than on previous trips to Croke Park, and having watched from the stands, the memories are still crystal clear. "It has been written as a wonderful All-Ireland with great football, particularly that spell for fifteen minutes in the second half. It was mesmerising and it knocked the heart out of Kildare. What people liked about the football, and about Gaelic football in general, was that is was such a clean game. You hardly needed a referee there at all. It was played with great spirit. And Kildare as well, they played it in that spirit. They are great sportspeople the Kildare people, and I chatted with a lot of them afterwards. People didn't expect that much of Galway. They were a fairly new team whereas Kildare had been there over the last decade. Some of them had been in Leinster finals and in some very serious games in Croke Park. One felt they had the experience, men like Glen Ryan and Anthony Rainbow. That half-back line was superb. And I must confess that I worried about the the strength of their defence. I knew that our strength was in the forwards, but the important thing for forwards is to get the quality ball in. And the ball they got from midfield was exceptionally good. Seán Ó Domhnaill laid off his passes. I don't think he put a foot wrong. Kevin Walsh, he moved out to the wing in the second half and he caught three or four catches from the kick-outs and he laid it off long and low.

"And then you had the likes of Michael Donnellan being able to come back into defence, carry the ball out of it, give it and being fit and speedy enough to take it on the run again and set up scores. The score that Seán Óg de Paor got in the first half, you had Michael Donnellan getting it in near the full-back line and he passed a ball to Kevin Walsh and ran again. By the time Kevin had collected the ball and turned he was gone by him, took the pass, soloed, gave it to Derek Savage and he passed it out to de Paor coming up to put it over the bar. That score emphasised what this Galway team were made of. In the second half there were great scores, like the one Ja Fallon got from the sideline. In fact, the one that he scored with his left foot from the left wing was even a more acute angle. For a left-footer it was a great score. Then there was the set-up for the goal. Again, that came from a long pass. John Divilly gave a very quick pass which carried up fifty yards to

Michael Donnellan. He collected it cleanly, gave it immediately inside and Padraic Joyce took his goal by just side-stepping the keeper and putting it in the back of the net. I mean, there's an awful lot of skill in all that. And we knew there was a lot of skill there because those guys came up through Jarlaths and we've been watching them for a long time."

Having those good forwards made all the difference between winning and losing. "Johnny Hughes said to me before the All-Ireland 'you won't win an All-Ireland with a great back line but you'll win an All-Ireland with a great forward line'. And it was true in the sense when people compared the back line of, say, Johnny Hughes, Liam O'Neill and Tommy Joe Gilmore with others. Now all of them won All-Stars and if you compared them with other half-back lines that had won All-Irelands, you'd say they don't compare. But it was true for Johnny. Coming up to the All-Ireland he stressed that he thought Galway were going to win it because they had such a great forward line. And it turned out like that."

Another reason for Galway's rise is John O'Mahony. Mattie knows what life is like from the managerial vantage point, having been in charge of the Galway senior team himself from 1980 to 1983 that won a national league and a pair of Connacht titles. And O'Mahony, equipped with a proven track record, is, he believes, a shrewd addition. "Obviously he's very organised. John O'Mahony has a proven record. His record with Mayo, with Leitrim and with Galway is second to none. There is nobody that has his record and I know a lot of people in Mayo are awfully sorry they hadn't given him a few more years. I know friends of his in Ballaghaderreen who would love to have seen him bring Sam home and would die for Mayo winning an All-Ireland.

"There was a lot put at his disposal. I remember in my time as manager, money, we were told, was so scarce they could scarcely give a steak to the likes of Brian Talty and Gay McManus when they'd come a hundred miles. Now you have people who are skilled on organising money for a start. You have doctors, you have physiotherapists, you have the best people involved and there seems to be no scarcity of money. The big businesses are coming in behind football now. That wasn't so back twenty years ago. Maybe we didn't market it right. Maybe a few counties like Kerry and Dublin did and got the most out of it. But at the moment there seems to be no difficulty in getting money."

Much is made of Galway's youthful vigour in 1998. But Mattie himself won his first All-Ireland having just turned eighteen. 1956 marked his initial emergence on to the senior inter-county scene and it could not have worked out better. It was an outcome, however, hardly envisaged following

Galway's showing the previous year. "In '55, Roscommon beat Galway below in Castlebar and Galway were diabolical on a wet day. They looked so terrible nobody would say they would win a Connacht title, not to mind win an All-Ireland the following year. And inside twelve months there was a transformation and a few of us came on to the team. There were two of them from my own club, Jackie Coyle and Mick Greally. It was like a giant jigsaw and we went on to win the All-Ireland. But then you had outstanding players, the likes of Purcell and Stockwell. To play on a team with someone like Purcell was something else. I was only a young lad and I had Purcell playing in front of me. I was just in awe of him. He was like God because I had watched him when I was thirteen and fourteen and then I was playing with him at eighteen...that was something for me. And the same in defence. You'd a great half-back line - Jack Kissane, Mick Greally and Jack Mahon in the middle. Jack Mangan, our captain, was in goal - a great goalkeeper. You don't win without great players and you don't win with too many weaknesses. We had the footballers."

But success in 1956 failed to spark further All-Ireland glory that decade. Cork, whom Galway had beaten in the 1956 final, gained revenge in the 1957 semi-final. In 1958, Dublin, courtesy of a last minute point, also downed Galway in a semi-final. And in the 1959 final, Kerry had their homework done on Stockwell and Purcell and Galway, hindered by doubts over players just returned from injury, were unravelled. It marked the first of a pair of All-Ireland finals Mattie was to lose as a player. But the trauma of losing acted as a spur, an incentive to do better, especially the defeat in the 1963 final against Dublin. That reverse was the rock upon which the drive for the three-in-a-row was built. "We should have won in '63. There was a question of a line ball being given and from it came the goal. But I maintained that if we had won it in '63, we might not have won three-in-a-row because we had fellas on the team who were new to it. I don't think they appreciated what it was to combine as a team and they went out of that dressingroom in '63 as a team feeling so badly they never wanted to be beaten again. That was what you had to have on a team. I was a fierce competitor. I absolutely hated to lose."

Balance, according to Mattie, was the foundation for the three-in-a-row, a requirement that was helped somewhat by the emergence of a few players on the senior team following an All-Ireland minor win in 1960 over Cork. Come 1964, Noel Tierney ruled at full-back. John Donnellan patrolled at half-back with Sean Meade and Martin Newell. Mick Reynolds and Mick Garrett were ascendant in midfield. Up front, Cyril Dunne and Seamus Leydon operated on either side of Mattie at half-forward, and John Keenan,

Sean Cleary and Christy Tyrrell formed the firm at full-forward. Backboned by goalkeeper Johnny Geraghty, the right blend had been achieved and Galway were poised and ready to succeed.

"Noel Tierney must be the best full-back I've ever seen play. The corner-backs were very solid and there was a great goalkeeper. The corner-backs would let Tierney up for the ball, but he knew they would never let him down. They were in behind him, ready to pick it up. There was a great understanding. And then John Donnellan at half-back, John had the heart of a lion. Sean Meade was a great footballer who subdued his own skills in order to mark tightly. He didn't mind breaking the ball away or not coming up with the high catch so long as he subdued his opponent and stopped the attack. That was his motto always. He was always a better footballer than he sometimes looked. He was a great footballer when he played at club level and went up for the ball. Sean just played a certain type of game for the county and sometimes he was underestimated because he didn't go for the glamour catch. He went for the safety. And Newell was speed itself. Newell was as talented at soccer or rugby and played rugby afterwards for Connacht.

"We had a good midfield, Mick Reynolds and Garrett and then later Pat Donnellan and Jimmy Duggan. Jimmy was a skilful player. Pat Donnellan was like Michael in 1998. He maybe didn't have the same finesse as Michael but he had an engine just like him. He went way back in defence, soloed the length of the field and delivered well. Then our forward line united very well. Dunne and Leydon were either side of me. You looked for them on the move and you'd pass the ball about fourteen yards ahead of them. And at club level I used to find when I'd pass the ball half that distance ahead of a player they'd give out to me and say 'why didn't you pass it to me?'. They'd still be stationary, but Dunne and Leydon were very fast. And you had John Keenan at left-full, a great scorer. Sean Cleary took up great positions at full-forward, gave good passes, and Tyrrell was on the right wing. He was very fast, very tricky and picked off scores. We were a very balanced outfit."

Aside from winning the All-Irelands, the sixties were noted for the trips that Galway made abroad. At the time, New York automatically played in the national league final in a bid to cement the game's roots across The Atlantic. Playing two games on each visit, Galway enjoyed the expeditions, even though a win in 1965 was followed by a large defeat in 1967. "The trips were the icing on the cake really. O.K., you had won the All-Ireland and you had an All-Ireland medal, but the real fun was travelling to New York, Chicago and Boston and meeting the Irish. For me it was like going home. There were nine of us in the family and seven had settled in Boston. There was a colony of McDonaghs over there. It was like going home anytime I went there. There was great *craic* in New York. The football was kind of secondary, really. We did lose to New York on the last occasion, but we were up against refereeing decisions. And you were on a very tight, short, narrow pitch. There was no such thing as giving a ball fourteen yards in front of a forward. Gaelic Park was a shambles as far as a pitch was concerned. The whole centre was like a man with a bald head down the middle. There was no grass, only sand, and it was like a desert. I remember being brought down and my knees and elbows were cut on the first solo run I did. It was like playing on the road. But New York, it was the fun we were there for."

However, the trips were to play a part in Galway's eventual dethronement as All-Ireland champions in 1967. Just back from a five-week adventure that included America and an appearance at London's Wembley Stadium, Galway returned only a week-and-a-half in advance of their game against Mayo. Rest was needed. But time was against them, and designs on a four-in-a-row were quashed in Castlebar.

The defeat, however, could not diminish Galway's achievements during the sixties. Following in the footsteps of Noel Tierney in 1964 and Martin Newell in 1965, Mattie was chosen as *Texaco* Gaelic Footballer of the Year for 1966, an award that is much treasured. "That was really something, to be picked as the Footballer of the Year. It was a great distinction and it could have been given to several others on the team. At the presentation you mixed with men like Ronnie Delaney, who was at the table with me, and Tony O'Reilly. Jack Lynch then handed the prize over. Strangely enough, Tony O'Reilly spent the time talking about farming. That time we didn't have that much dairy farming and he was basically saying that Ireland was a great country for dairy farming and if we went out and sold our produce in Europe it would be second to none. It has all happened since."

With his playing days at an end, Mattie took his experience and eventually moved into the sphere of management, taking charge of Galway from 1980 to 1983. At the time, Roscommon were Connacht's premier county having just completed a four-in-a-row, but Galway were soon to change that. They trounced Roscommon in the 1981 national league final and although Mayo subsequently beat them in the Connacht championship, Mattie regrouped and guided Galway to provincial success in 1982 and 1983. The great Kerry All-Ireland four-in-a-row side was coming to the end of its dominance, so the potential to attain Sam Maguire victories was obvious. But it was not to be. Galway lost to eventual winners Offaly in a close-run semi-final in 1982 and followed it up in 1983 with an All-Ireland final defeat against Dublin.

Many opined that 1983 was Galway's year, their time to be crowned champions. But Mattie differs, reckoning the previous year is the one that got away. "1982 was the year we should have won it. We played Offaly in the semi-final and we played very well. But we had weaknesses and the weaknesses showed up. In the atmosphere of Croke Park we lost it a bit. But that was the year we had a good outfit. The following year a lot of the players were pushing on. It was a great team and I often felt that if I had that team in the seventies rather than the eighties, they would have been in several All-Irelands. We were just weak in spots. You might win against a poor team, but you don't win All-Irelands if you have too many weaknesses. We were a bit like Roscommon in 1980. They had great players like Tony McManus, but a few great players don't win it unfortunately. Our lads from the seventies - Johnny Hughes, Joyce and Talty - you would have loved to have seen them lads winning All-Irelands. They were great players, but unfortunately there were always those weaknesses elsewhere."

Galway may not have won an All-Ireland then, but Mattie's position amongst the echelons of great servants to Galway football remains untouched. His legacy is a testament to competing with a verve and a great will-to-win. It served him well and it is not forgotten. Firm evidence of this was seen as recently as last September. While the population of County Galway was in the throes of expressing adulation to a new generation of All-Ireland winners, Mattie once more became a focus of attention. Adults, to whom he was a childhood hero, were sending their own children and grandchildren over for a brief audience and a treasured autograph.

It was unexpected recognition, but it says a lot about the aura of Mattie McDonagh. A football legend.

*   *   *   *

Tommy Joe Gilmore, The Searching Seventies

Sport can often be a cruel concoction, blessing those of adequate talent with the greatest of riches and leaving others who ooze indisputable greatness to shoulder too much suffering. An indictment of the fates, its effect is sometimes hard to rationalise. When finals are lost it is often said, in a bid to boost morale, that a team must lose a final before it gets to win one. But that popular myth was nothing only a hoary old notion, a flawed maxim when used in conjunction with the Galway Gaelic footballers of the seventies. Convention had it that the reaching of three finals in a four year phase would procure the ultimate reward. Not so. On each occasion the elusive medals looked reachable but their receipt was to be thwarted. It was a bum deal. Offaly were the culprits in 1971. Cork followed suit in 1973 and Dublin, unquestionably Galway's bogey team in championship fare, acted as spoilsports in 1974.

Croke Park was not the sweetest of Meccas back then for players of a Western disposition. Galway held a round the clock vigil in pursuit of the title. All things being equal they were bound to come through and eventually take one. Instead their hopes proved forlorn and the unstinting quest for All-Ireland medals became a cruel, wild goose chase. In particular, heartstrings tugged for nine Galway personnel who played in the three finals. Admittedly, two players were a throwback to the successful 1966 side. Both Liam Sammon and Colie McDonagh, medals pocketed, were vestiges of a bygone era when success was an annual harvest. But the other seven were never to be ordained. They were made to settle for the trimmings, a haul of Connacht titles.

Of the seven, one of Galway's most predatory performers was Tommy Joe Gilmore. A player of great muscular build, the defensive bulwark had genuine qualifications to believe that his granite-like presence would reap the nirvana of an All-Ireland win. The collective will of the half-back partnership he struck-up with Johnny Hughes, in all three years, and with Liam O'Neill, in the latter two, was deeply engraved on the minds of opponents and greatly respected by them in the heat and dust of battle. The trio were bestowed All-Star awards for their dependability, but the gong long hankered for never materialised. One last roll of the dice, in 1983 with Tommy, a sub, and Johnny, starting, foundered against Dublin once more to leave the half-back ensemble to exit centrestage without a victorious splurge.

Throughout it all Tommy, now a 48-year-old, took the setbacks on the chin. His Croke Park memoirs might not make pretty reading. He even played on losing Connacht Railway Cup final sides at headquarters. Yet he remains pragmatic about the whole experience. A pair of All-Star awards, achieved back-to-back in 1972 and 1973, and a national league medal sit pretty with a hoard of Connacht titles. But no matter how strong a defence is, forwards are what is required to win All-Ireland finals. That was proven in 1998 as it was the good form of the Galway attackers which made the decisive difference against Kildare. But back to the seventies. In two of the three finals, in 1971 and 1974, Galway, leading and looking strong, scented Sam Maguire could be theirs. Titillated by being so close, they came a cropper when accuracy was needed up front. Not accepting chances hastened their downfall on those occasions. But ironically the one final in which events ran smoothly in attack and Galway scored 2-13, their defence, conceding 3-17, was at fault. That 2-13 tally continues to be the highest ever scored by a losing side in an All-Ireland final. Yet it is a statistic which offers mere consolation. If only Galway were not so patchy and had instead produced the right blend of reliable scoring prowess and adequate defending on any given All-Ireland day, the seventies might not have been so barren in Croke Park.

Reflecting on the seventies in the joyous aftermath of Galway's 1998 triumph, Tommy agrees that there could well have been no thirty two year gap for John O'Mahony's men to bridge. "Being in three finals in four years you were very close to it. I honestly think we certainly should have won two out of three. If we took our chances in '71 against Offaly, we could have won. Now whether we were a better team in the overall picture I don't know. But on the day we should have taken it. We missed a lot of chances from placed balls, frees that were scoreable. Certainly, I can remember going in with a five point lead against Offaly at half-time. We had something like five or six frees missed inside thirty and thirty five metres that were scoreable. Offaly had a guy on their side who was kicking fifties and forty fives. That was the difference. We lost by about three points in the end, but they were the chances you had got to take. You've got to have the forwards, you've got to put the points on the board. That's what wins games for you. I'm a firm believer in that. You can defend all you like, but if you're not scoring at the other end the ball is coming back on top of you again.

"We met a Cork team in '73 that were really a good side. They should possibly have won another one. We wouldn't have a lot of big qualms about that one. But certainly the one again in '74, the one against Dublin. A lot of people talk about the missed penalty (Dublin's Paddy Cullen saved Sammon's spot-kick), but we had three other good goal chances besides the penalty. Penalties are fifty-fifty, but the pressure is on the taker. That was another game we left behind us again by not taking our chances."

Twenty four years on though, Ireland was treated to an exhibition of score-taking by a team wearing the maroon. Their players displayed a bulging pride in the jersey, a respect that mirrored a similar characteristic shown by Tommy when he was incumbent in the number six top. It was an event for celebratory emotions to be revealed and Tommy, a Galway selector in 1997 when Val Daly was in charge, was no exception. "It was emotional, particularly for a fella like myself who played the game, who played in three finals and was on the losing side. The past was sort of buried. It was a day that I will always remember, especially having known the lads from last year. I knew they were quite capable of delivering the goods. The game itself started quite well for Galway for fifteen minutes, but there was a bit of a lull for the remainder of the half. Then it just totally exploded in the second half. It was a tremendous performance by everybody. The game was over about seven minutes into the second half.

"It was very pleasing that Galway gave a performance of pure football - from good high fielding, long accurate kicking to great long range point-taking. All that is what's good about football. That's what Gaelic football is about. It would have been the type of football we played in the seventies. The difference was this year these lads put the ball over the bar. And that's what you have to do to win it. It was pleasing. When the final whistle went it was great to see the All-Ireland had come West and I was particularly pleased that it had come to Galway naturally enough. It was a thirty two year gap. I was there as a sixteen-year-old in 1966 and you didn't think you'd have to wait that long to see it again."

Tommy's stint as a selector came to an end when Mayo plundered Tuam in May 1997 to win a provincial first round tie by four points. Starting disastrously and falling an unanswered 1-4 behind after just ten minutes, Galway doggedly fought back to lead 0-12 to 1-7 ten minutes into the second half. It looked promising, but their catch-up exertions had drained energy reserves and a second Mayo spurt proved insurmountable for Galway. It was a setback to lofty aspirations, yet it could not hide the talented framework inherent within the team. And that talent flourished in 1998.

"Most of the players were there last year. The two players that weren't there were Jarlath Fallon and Kevin Walsh. Both were injured and they were a big influence on the team this year. They're two of the more senior players on the panel and if we had them last year, things could have been different. But that's football. If you have them, you have them. If you haven't, you have to do without them. They certainly would have been a big boost to us. That doesn't take away from this year. I knew the talent was there. Myself,

Val Daly and Gerry Fahy did a lot of work and put a lot of effort into last year. The nucleus of the team was there, but John O'Mahony, Peter Warren and Stephen Joyce certainly built on that. With all due respects to them, they did a very professional job and left no stone unturned. All credit to them."

On the playing front, Tommy points to several contributions that were of utmost importance. They include that of his own Cartoon Shamrocks club colleague, Derek Savage, Tomás Mannion, Seán Ó Domhnaill, Walsh, Michael Donnellan and Fallon. But remembering what was central to Galway's downfall in the seventies, Tommy has special praise for the accurate, cold blooded free-taking, in particular Padraic Joyce's effort that brought the curtain down on the first half of the final. "You have to take the scores, especially free-taking. You get a free inside the forty five, you've got to get two out of three of those over the bar at least. Any team that doesn't do that doesn't win. But Galway did. A typical one would be the point before half-time, that Padraic Joyce free. There was four points in it and he got the free. It wasn't easy, it was at an angle. But he slotted it and it left a kick of the ball between them. These are the frees you've got to take, the scores you've got to be taking to win All-Irelands."

Aside from witnessing a Connacht team live up to expectation on final day at Croke Park, the extra competitiveness within the province is another feature of recent years. "There's no easy game in the championship now. Leitrim have become a force to be reckoned with, have been over the last six or seven years. Sligo have been making steady progress. And Roscommon, of course. were really the dark horses this year and nearly could have won a Connacht final. I actually think it prepared Galway for Croke Park and made a better team of them. It's certainly going to make for an interesting Connacht championship next year with Galway as All-Ireland champions. Everybody is going to be wanting to take them. And certainly Mayo, they'll really fancy their chances. It certainly will lift the whole thing in Connacht. That's a good thing."

While All-Ireland reward eluded Tommy, individual recognition came his way aplenty. Launched in 1971 to great accord were the All-Star awards, a scheme devised to pay due recognition on an annual basis to the country's fifteen most eminent footballers. Revelling in his prime, Tommy duly collected awards for his contributions in 1972 and 1973. Even the hindrance of having a leg in a plaster of Paris following a knee injury failed to deter Tommy from collecting the first award. "It was a fantastic night, a great achievement and a great honour for any player to be given an All-Star. They're a very personal achievement. They're nice, but you would give ten All-Stars just to have one All-Ireland medal. The All-Ireland medal is the one. After that, whatever comes is a bonus. That's the way I looked at it. Certainly the awards were nice. They were some consolation prizes, let's say, but the ultimate is the All-Ireland medal."

Currently not actively involved in the game, Tommy, through his job as a sales rep, continually ventures throughout County Galway. Even though it has been a while since he played, his existence is still defined by people referring to him as Tommy Joe Gilmore - Galway footballer. "It's amazing all the people who would say 'you did well, you'd a great year'. People sort of associate you with football all the time, even though you're not involved or anything. People do associate you with it. They always will, I suppose, which is a nice thing."

Sure is. Especially for a respected double All-Star.

5

The Early Years

John O'Mahony's earliest footballing memories were of his Cork-born father leaving for the long journey to Croke Park to see the Leesiders take on the eventual winners Louth in the 1957 All-Ireland football. The four-year-old boy waving off his football loving Dad was in the early stages of developing what would turn out to be a hugely successful involvement in the world of Gaelic football.

It was the pull of work that brought his father, Stephen O'Mahony, to the West and eventually to Dohertys grocery store in Lisacul where his future wife, Bridget Gallagher from Belmullet, worked. Bridget eventually interviewed Stephen for a job at the store, a romance blossomed and marrying in 1951, they purchased a house in Magheraboy, on the outskirts of Ballaghaderreen in East Mayo.

Three years after the late, great Sean Flanagan captained Mayo to the first of their two-in-a-row All-Ireland success in 1950, Stephen and Bridget O'Mahony, living on the edge of Sean's home town, had their second child, John on June 8th, 1953. It would not be long before their middle son would be associating himself with a game that Mayo had become masters of at the start of the fifties.

As the legs began to stretch, young John and his friends would leave well-worn tracks as they played ball on the field at the back of his house in Magheraboy. The house, as John describes it, was the "last house in Mayo", located mere yards away from the Roscommon border. A few short steps brought you into a different county, a different diocese and a different footballing allegiance. Not suprisingly, the appreciation of Mayo football became more pronounced as he got older.

Primary schools football was an invention yet to come when John was growing up but his first taste of organised football came in the form of a regular three mile journey to the sportsfield in Kilmovee. Many Sunday afternoons were whiled away by young lads with plenty of dreams bouncing around in their lively minds. And the fact that there were three sons in the family ensured that the talk of football and sport was never far away from their thoughts. "There were three of us, Dan, myself and Stephen, so it was a male-dominated household and I suppose that's where the football came from." There were countless times when he and his buddies would take out the ball straight after Mass on a Sunday and play marathon kick-abouts. The memories are still clear of 'being as stiff as a board the next day'.

Recollections of his father travelling to the 1957 All-Ireland are hazy but even as a youngster, the memories of listening, watching, and going to matches are still relatively unblurred. With Stephen senior always keen to get to as many big games as he could, the journeys would sometimes involve young John if the all-important car wasn't bulging at the seams. "My father used to go to all the Connacht championship matches. It was the tradition at the time where the few local men would gather together. There wouldn't be too many with cars and you'd head off in a full car. For one game, the crowd in the car was too big and I remember being disappointed that I couldn't go.

There are other childhood memories too that are still fresh in the mind. "I remember my first Connacht championship, it was in 1962 and I'm nearly sure it was in Tuam between Galway and Mayo. We were behind the goals and I can still picture that. I was nine at the time and I wasn't able to follow the game. You just looked at the ball that came into the goal. I think looking back, you would say that a nine-year-old nowadays knows more about the game now than a nine-year-old in the early sixties. I didn't know the importance of it then and I didn't know who won it that day or which side was playing who the next day. But I do remember the famous games between Roscommon and Sligo in Charlestown and going to those. It was the year of the broken crossbar."

Early dabbles with football became more structured when 13-year-old John entered the reputed St. Nathys as a boarding student. It marked the beginning of five academic years which gave him educational qualifications to make his mark in life. It also proved a fertile bed for a young man whose love for football became a consuming passion. John's eldest brother Dan had become a St. Nathys student two years earlier and, not surprisingly, his brother's involvement in the college's football scene was to provide further interest for the first-year student.

"When I went to St. Nathys, it was the first opportunity to play on a team and I didn't play on any organised team before that. My older brother Dan was playing football there. I went there in 1966, and to get on the juvenile team in first year was the ambition straight-away."

His first taste of life in the green college jersey was between the sticks. "I was probably not good enough to get on outfield, I was a kind of stopper, you know. I saw being in goals as a case of being delighted to play anywhere. It was also kind of unusual that not too many first years would be on the team. There was no first-year competition at the time and I remember the first match, playing against Muiredeachs down in Tubbercurry. It started from there and in second year, I won a Connacht juvenile medal and I played full-back that year."

John's solid physique ensured that he soon became a key figure in many of the college teams' defences in the following years. The full-back line became his second home and his qualities were tailor-made for the direct and no-nonsense style that characterised football in those years. "I was strong, a one hundred per cent player and I was totally passionate about the game. I wouldn't have much going for me if I hadn't the bit of passion and grit. I wasn't the most skilful but football was different that time. Basically, if you were playing full-back or corner-back, you got the ball and you kicked it as far as you could.

"I won an All-Ireland minor medal with Mayo in 1971 and I got one kick of the ball in the final. Football was definitely different then. It was a more static game. If you kicked a ball into the corner-forward, the right corner-back or left corner-back would be there, more or less, so there was less mobility. There was no question of playing a third midfielder or a twin full-forward line. Tactics would be minimal and I suppose that changed with the Dublin/Kerry thing."

1968 is a year that stands out like a beacon on St. Nathys' roll-call of honour. Connacht titles in juvenile, junior and senior grades mark a historic achievement but there is more than a tinge of regret that a brilliant senior team did not bring back the Hogan Cup like their 1957 predecessors. They are times that John, then a second year who had an unsuccessful trial with that team, remembers all too well. "One of my sporting highlights was the memory of '68 when St. Nathys should have won an All-Ireland senior title. I was a second year at the time and I remember being brought out for an unsuccessful trial as a sub-goalie but my brother Dan played on that team. Coláiste Chriost Rí from Cork beat them in the All-Ireland semi-final replay after extra-time. The drawn game was played in Portlaoise and the whole school went to it. It was on a Palm Sunday and we were on our Easter holidays.

"The replay took place when were back in school and we didn't get to it. I remember waiting for the result. It wasn't like now when you had local radio covering it and at six or half-six, a phone-call came to the school to say we had lost. We got a radio then at quarter-to-seven to hear the sports report. Chriost Rí went on to win the final by twelve or thirteen points." Ironically, one of the team members was former Mayo and Roscommon player, Sean

Kilbride, a selector on the current Roscommon senior team. John's collection of college medals - one Connacht juvenile (1968) and two Connacht junior (1968 and 1970, the latter year as captain) - was not followed by senior provincial honours. The nearest opportunity came in 1969 when St. Nathys were defeated by St. Marys in the Connacht final.

Football may have been a growing pre-occupation but there were other matters of a more spiritual nature that were equally at the forefront of his mind. St. Nathys religious and spiritual ethos encouraged their young men to consider a religious life and John was no different to the many who had contemplated such a vocation. "I went to Maynooth College where I spent two years as a clerical student. There would have been a culture of thinking about the priesthood and there would have been a few class-mates that went as well." John was one of five contemporaries who entered the seminary, a group that included former Sligo great, Paddy Henry, but only one, Joe Caulfield, completed his studies for the priesthood.

An Arts degree was acquired, but, in between the academic pursuits, football was still top of the agenda at Maynooth. One of the highlights was being part of a surprise packet of a senior team that laid down some big markers against the more traditional powers. "There was a huge interest in football at the time when Maynooth College was just opening up. Maynooth played in their first Sigerson Cup in '72 when I was in second year. I was on that team and we were beaten the following year by U.C.D. in a fantastic final. They had a team of inter-county players with the likes of John O'Keeffe and Kevin Kilmurray in their ranks."

The inter-county scene at this time was also not foreign to John. He had been a member of the Mayo minor team that won an All-Ireland in 1971 after defeating a Cork team that contained a lanky figure called Jimmy Barry-Murphy. His Alma Mater never veered out of view though and he was back teaching there in 1975, just three years after completing his Leaving Certificate. With a higher diploma in teaching from U.C.G. tucked under his arm, he became one of the new staff members recruited during the St. Nathys' expansion scheme.

Footballing matters immediately began to consume his extra-curricular activities. Work with college teams dovetailed with his Ballaghaderreen involvement. Those early years as a teacher coincided with the success of the local club which enjoyed its best ever spell, winning a first and only senior county title in 1972. John was a member of that team, a 19-year-old student playing at corner-back. "That was a great era for club football in Ballaghaderreen. We won a minor title in the late sixties and won an intermediate and senior in the early seventies."

His football career was now peaking on many fronts. Following the 1971 minor success, he went on to represent the county in the U-21 grade. There was much disappointment at losing to Kerry in the 1973 All-Ireland final but it was more than offset the following year when he captured honours at that grade when Antrim were defeated in the final after a replay. His contribution to the success was rewarded with a series of championship and league appearances on the county senior team between 1972 and 1975. "My best period of football at senior level was around the time when we won the senior club title in 1972. I remember playing Galway in a Gael Linn match after that and I cleaned up. But I wasn't a very versatile player and I don't think I would have survived in the nineties."

Unfortunately, his ambitions of securing a regular place came during a soul-searching period for Mayo football and it is not recorded as one of their most fruitful. From 1972 to 1975, Mayo played in and lost three Connacht finals. John played at corner-back in the 1973 final ("I did o.k."), was exam-tied for the following year's championship and had a bit part in the 1975 provincial final, which Sligo won after a replay. Attempts at breaking into the team ended up with broken dreams.

"My ambition was to be a regular on the senior team. We had won an All-Ireland U-21 title in 1974 and automatically there was eleven of that team on the senior team the following year when we lost to Sligo. But it was a difficult transient period when a lot of players were coming and going. I would love to have completed the collection of Connacht medals. I had a minor, U-21 and I would have loved to have got a Connacht senior but I didn't. I was dropped, if you like, after the '75 final but basically what I did get involved in was coaching teams in the club and we won an East Mayo title in '76, so that filled the void."

It may have been a transitional time for Mayo and John's aspirations as an inter-county footballer may have been short-lived but it was also the embryonic period of his coaching career. At a time when he was a regular on the club senior team, he gradually became immersed in managing club and college teams. The role of leader and co-ordinator is something that always appealed to him. Even as a student when he was senior house captain, he always enjoyed the responsibility that came with leadership and taking the initiative - qualities that would prove crucial for many teams in the following decades. "I must have enjoyed that whole thing in college in the sense that if we were kicking in and out of goals on a field, well then I'd say 'let's do something constructive here', so maybe it came in that way."

Apart from his inaugural management success with a minor club team in 1976, the teacher, in his early twenties, soon found himself drawn to the needs of the senior set-up within the club. "I would have been helping out with club senior teams but not actually managing them because I was playing. I did a bit of training with them and stuff like that and I'd have a certain input in the way of making comments on tactics or whatever. I think I would be the type of guy that takes to that kind of responsibility. I was player-manager in '77, the year that the great team broke up. John Morley went to Castlerea and a few players like Sean Kilbride, Frank Burns, Johnny McKenzie and Jim Fleming had gone off the scene.

"When I became involved, the team was all around the one age and I kind of took over the reins a bit. I wouldn't have had the title of player-manager but I was teaching in the college, living at home and organising the training. Again, it was the thing of taking responsibility. It would have come that way rather than a conscious decision to take over the team. We got to a county semi-final that year but someone else then took control and I faded back because I didn't want to be mixing it that much with the playing side of things."

A Connacht senior championship title had already eluded him, a senior club title didn't but John, during the mid-seventies, hankered for more senior club honours. They didn't materialise. "I was nineteen when we won our first senior in '72 so you didn't appreciate it. You were thinking at that age you'd be back to win more, but it didn't work out like that. The nearest we got was back in '85 when were beaten in the final by Ballina."

Even though still in his late twenties, his reputation as a trainer and coach with college and club teams began to have a ripple effect. In 1982, his name came to the attention of Liam O'Neill, who was manager of the Mayo U-21 side. It was then that the beginning of his career as an inter-county manager entered its formative stages. "In 1982, I coached an U-21 club team that got to a county final. At that time, Liam O'Neill was in charge of the Mayo U-21 team and he was stepping up to senior. So, he recommended me for the position. I never really thought about it, I really didn't. The club was my only thing at the time. I was a bit apprehensive but I still would have taken to it and enjoyed it. It came as a surprise to me and then when I became manager, I wanted to do well. At that time, the U-21 competition was played throughout the summer, so we didn't have to get organised until maybe April or May."

Unknown to him then, those two seasons with the U-21 team set in chain a driving desire to equip himself with all the latest training developments that were changing the complexion of Gaelic football. That change was reflected by the emergence of the great Kerry and Dublin teams who had discarded the static patterns for a fluid, unshackled brand of football.

With the promptings of the County Board, John attended a number of national coaching courses comprising some of the best known and most regarded personnel in the game. The insights proved invaluable. "Around that time, I would have done a coaching course in Gormanstown for a week during the summer of '83. When I went there, I was really intrigued by it. Mickey Sullivan, Mickey Whelan, Brian McEniff were some of the speakers and we went out to the Dublin training sessions. We talked to them about the players and how they approached big games and things like that. I would have been taken by that coaching thing. There was no great audio-visual stuff that time but I found the talks and lecturers very interesting. I found it was original, it was new to me. I went back to a number of them because I enjoyed it and had a hunger for that kind of thing. In the middle of that, we won the U-21 All-Ireland title and that copper-fastened my interest in coaching."

That title was hard-earned following a replay against Derry but John has special memories of a team that worked extremely hard as a unit. "That was a good team. There was a togetherness about them and a lot of them were coming through to senior and Noel Durkin, who had not played minor for Mayo, ended up as man of the match in the '83 final. We had a good set of players, we worked very hard with them and they were very committed. Winning the All-Ireland in your first year was certainly special."

Incredible success in his first year preceded a marvellous run to another All-Ireland final the very next season. Cork punctured those aspirations, however, and John subsequently decided to step down. It was time to refresh his ideas. "I wanted a break but I would have loved to have taken those guys when they won a senior in '85. I would have loved to have got a chance to have taken them," he says of a Liam O'Neill-trained team that was subsequently beaten in an All-Ireland semi-final replay by Dublin.

The big chance did come two years later at the age of thirty four when he was appointed senior team manager in the wake of O'Neill's resignation. There was a two-year break hitherto but that interim period between his U-21 involvement and his first dip into the waters of senior inter-county management was spent attending coaching courses and developing further insights into the game. "I intended to take those kind of breaks anyway, time-out to keep refreshed but there again I'm talking about myself - in all that time and in all my time in management, there always has been good people with me."

John's management team consisted of four other selectors, County Board chairman at the time Mick Higgins, Charlie Collins, the late Christy O'Haire and the late Seamie Daly. It was no secret that John, from the outset, never enjoyed the five-man selector system and the difficulties that arose from that are well documented. "At the time, I had no choice with my selectors. They were picked by delegates. I have had the system of three since and I would never go back to the five situation."

Whatever of his reservations, one of the selectors, above all of them, became a seismic influence in shaping the evolving managerial career of John O'Mahony. "I was lucky that I had Seamie Daly from Mulranny who trained and managed the Mayo team to win the league in 1970. He was the perfect gentleman and he was fantastic to me. Here was a guy who won a national title with Mayo and had been associated in some way with every Connacht title that Mayo had won since the fifties. He trained the Mayo team in the sixties and was involved as a player. He was injured in 1950 and '51 but he was involved with the '48 team (beaten by Cavan in the All-Ireland final) that was commemorated recently. When Mayo won Connacht titles in 1967 and '69, he was manager. After winning the league with the '70 team, he was manager in '81. The only team he wasn't involved with was the '85 team and then he was back in '88 and '89. He would have been the pulse of Mayo football over thirty or forty years.

"At inter-county level, he would have been my biggest influential figure. I learned a lot from him about how to deal with people. In 1987, he would have been in his early seventies but he was still very sharp and he had a great relationship with the younger players. He never tried to undermine me and was totally loyal to me. He never tried to impose himself in a big way but he always was a guiding hand to me. I will be eternally grateful to him. He would have been one of the four or five people that came into my mind when Galway won the All-Ireland last September."

There may have been a reservoir of talent from the 1983 U-21 team which became the backbone of O'Mahony's team during his period with Mayo. But the challenge at the outset was trying to blend that with the resources remaining after the fragmentation of a talented 1985 team. In any case, it proved to be a baptism of fire for the new Mayo manager but ironically, the season ended in perfect fashion. "Mayo won the Connacht title in 1985 but lost out in '86 and '87. They had put in a huge effort and there was a break-up of focus and it was a matter of trying to get that back together again. Funnily enough, we lost five league games after Christmas, got relegated but we still won the Connacht championship."

Despite the beginning of a new order, Mayo still had the makings of a promising team, easily disposing of Roscommon in the 1988 provincial final. However, the disappointment against defending champions Meath in the All-Ireland semi-final was a huge lesson for John and the players, one that stood them in good stead the following year. "I remember that Meath were way ahead of us, leading by ten or twelve points. In the last twenty minutes we got back at them. We got within four points and Liam McHale had a goal disallowed. I wondered what would it have been like if we had a cut at them from the outset, so we went with that kind of motivation into the '89 championship."

The 1989 season also marked the beginning of a radical dismantling of existing perceptions about Connacht football. "You would have felt that there were possibilities of winning with them but at that time, the ethos in Connacht was that a Connacht title was almost an end in itself. I don't know why that was. If you won a provincial title, you were almost successful. You felt something more needed to be done."

U-21 All-Ireland graduates, such as John Finn, Noel Durkin, John Maughan, Sean Maher, Kevin McStay and Peter Forde, mixed with the leadership of the more senior members, T.J. Kilgallon, Dermot Flanagan and Willie Joe Padden, was proof positive that the Mayo team of the late eighties had huge potential. John was convinced of that rich promise, a belief that was substantiated by his deep knowledge of the players. "I felt that I had an understanding with those guys. After that semi-final against Meath, I felt we had achieved as much as we could have so I set about trying to make sure that we did not see winning a Connacht title as an end in itself the following year."

There was also the added incentive of winning back-to-back titles in 1989 for the first time in thirty eight years. That statistic almost remained in the dusty files before Mayo triumphed following a thrilling two-match epic with Roscommon in the Connacht final. The intensity of that mammoth challenge stood the team in good stead and there was a renewed sense of vigour and anticipation about Mayo football after the All-Ireland semi-final when they dismissed a rated Tyrone team, comprising many of the side that played in the 1986 All-Ireland final. It was one of the more professional displays delivered by a Connacht team at Croke Park in those times.

The All-Ireland final against Cork and the heroics of the Mayo team, in which a tightly contested game ended with the Leesiders finishing stronger in the final straight, were hugely enthralling but ultimately disappointing. That defeat, however, did not stop one of Connacht's best performances in an All-Ireland final in decades sparking off near mass hysteria in the county. It is something that John still looks on with a great degree of unease. There was no Sam Maguire but players attained celebrity status. "I was gutted by the defeat in '89. That year, there were seven thousand people in Knock waiting for us. It was an unreal feeling. The goodwill was great and the people were very genuine but we were being celebrated and we had nothing to celebrate. All you were saying to the supporters was 'we'll do it next year'. We fully intended to I suppose but all over that winter, the players were kind of treated as celebrities. I felt uneasy about it but you felt you would have got it back on track." 1990 was ripe for a fall. Six of that All-Ireland team went on an All-Star tour in May ahead of an impending championship semi-final clash against Galway, a number of key players were injured and John felt the mood was not properly focused for defending the title. Galway won by two points, ensuring an early and sobering championship exit.

Sharp lessons were learnt from that defeat and the Tribesmen felt the sting in the 1991 championship semi-final when subjected to a thirteen point hiding. Optimism levels more than flickered again ahead of the provincial decider against title-holders Roscommon. A return to glory looked on the cards in Castlebar but young Derek Duggan's 'mother-of-all frees' forced a replay that ended in severe disappointment.

Not surprisingly, the wheels of the 1989 rollercoaster had now grinded to a halt and knives were being sharpened. John needed little prompting in making the decision to step down. "It was my biggest disappointment, bigger than '90 really. In the circumstances, I decided to walk away." The departure was made more painful with the publicised difference of opinions between him and certain people over the selector system. Reflecting back, however, there was still a sense of satisfaction that the episode led to a change in the system after his departure.

"I was unhappy with the five-man selection system. I wanted to hand-pick a small amount of people. Looking at it afterwards, I was glad that it happened. I was refused that option but the next people to come in '92 weren't. I would look at it as something that happened that made a difference. The irony of the thing is that Mayo could have won an All-Ireland in '92 but for a bit of upheaval."

Despite the ending, the achievements and the friendships forged over those years as Mayo senior team manager are something he will always treasure. "The memories of that time are precious. I would have great friends in the County Board and I still have great friendships with a lot of the players. There would have been regrets that we didn't win an All-Ireland title. I felt I made a bit of a mark. To a certain extent, there was a sense of fulfilment but you would still be kind of saying what might have been. I didn't want to become a good manager that had never won an All-Ireland title but I didn't see myself at that stage of having an opportunity to put that right.

"I would have had differences with individual people but when I finished my time with Mayo, some people would have said to me 'you'll be back with Mayo again at some stage'. I would have felt 'no, I've done my stint'. I also would have had no major ambition to go to any other county and I can say that with hand on heart."

The severing of his ties as manager of Mayo looked set to be a defining moment in John's sporting life. It was the end of his inter-county management career. Or so he thought at the time.

6

Leitrim Love Affair

It was the infectious enthusiasm of a County Board and a willing bunch of players that persuaded John to take on the mission of transforming the fortunes of Leitrim football. To some, it may have been a strange journey, even a risky venture to undertake. But it was a challenge that the Mayo man could not ultimately ignore.

1992 was an enjoyable year for John. Taking time out from the pressurised world of management, he took up the invitation to be a match analyst for a local radio station. Dissecting games is something that he naturally loved and the fact that he could do it in a much more open and objective fashion added to the enjoyment. He also still played the odd a bit of football and had certain club commitments but in the autumn of that year, his football sabbatical, unknown to him at the time, was ticking away quickly when the opportunity to manage Leitrim suddenly appeared on the horizon.

"The Leitrim thing came out of the blue. Tony McGowan (Leitrim County Board Chairman) rang me about it. It was a strange kind of feeling because I would be very Mayo and people would know that. I would never have seen a situation where I would go to another county. There had been some speculation that Eugene McGee was going to Leitrim at the time. I said 'Tony, give it to one of the other names you have'. I said 'I don't want to insult you but I have no ambition to get involved'. I said 'I can't see myself going outside my own county'. I said to him 'if I had to give you an answer now, it would have to be no'."

Leitrim were not prepared to give up easily and it was clear that, despite the other contenders, John O'Mahony was the number one choice. Gradually, the initial promptings turned into discussions and after a series of meetings, which included the players, he simply could not resist the opportunity of working with such a determined group of people. He was also well aware of the good foundations laid by his predecessor, P.J. Carroll. "I met the chairman, Tony McGowan, secretary Tommie Moran and vice-chairman Eamon Tubman. I was taken by their enthusiasm when I met them in the sense they were determined that something could be won. I asked to meet a few of the players to find out what their feelings were. We met them a few days afterwards and they came across so enthusiastic - I'm a glutton for punishment in that way. But, to be honest, I was taken by it from both players and officials. And I found myself within a week saying 'Yeah, I'll have a cut at this'. I wanted to be sure that it was the right thing to do and talking to my personal friends, I would have driven to Carrick-on-Shannon, driven to the places they trained and looked at the pitches."

Combined with a renowned personalised touch, his meticulous and intense preparations with Mayo had earned him widespread respect. It was the same approach that he wanted to inculcate among his new players. "I found it a lovely new challenge when I was in there. It was fresh and enthusiastic and, basically, I think they would have seen me as a person who would have won a Connacht title. I said to them that once I decided to go for this, 'it was the full hog and that's what I want from them. There was no half-measures'."

The players responded magnificently during his four-year tenure, one which saw a series of negative statistics about Leitrim football blown out of the water. Ojective one was to get out of the quagmire of Division Three. John's first game in charge was a league victory over Longford. It was a good start but he did find the adaptation somewhat unusual at the outset. No red and green jerseys anymore. "It was a bit strange. The dressing-room was all mustard." Despite a heavy defeat at the hands of All-Ireland champions Donegal, a morale-boosting draw against Cork and a steady accumulation of points guaranteed promotion to Division Two. Confidence was now beating steadily in Leitrim chests but the lack of championship progress for many years still did not inspire supporters to be hailing a new dawn.

A first round summer meeting against Galway, who they had not beaten in forty four years of championship football, represented an arduous challenge, though the Tribesmen, still looking for a provincial breakthrough since 1987, were going through a recession of their own. Nevertheless, the confidence generated in the league and John's ethos of unwavering self-belief combined to produce a wonderful victory. After going four points behind early in the second half, they went on to rally magnificently. Inspired by the promptings of George Dugdale at centre-forward, four unanswered points followed before a Jarlath Fallon point squared the game in the closing stages.

Leitrim's trump card, however, came in the dying embers and John fondly reminisces about that historic day. "It was a very disciplined display.

We beat them with an Aidan Rooney point in the last minute and I can still see the winner - Pat Donoghue catching in the middle of the field, the ball going to Colin McGlynn and Aidan Rooney kicking it over the bar. That was a momentous victory in the sense that it was forty something years since Leitrim had done that before.

"It was a great irony at the time - one of these great hoodoos, or supposed hoodoos, that Mayo couldn't win in Tuam and the first time I went with Leitrim we cracked it. I had drawn with Mayo in Tuam when I managed them but I never won, so it was gas really." The enormity of the victory for Leitrim people soon began to dawn on him. "It was a huge win for Leitrim. I didn't realise the extent of it until the next day when I picked up, I think it was the *Irish Press*, and there was a picture of Mickey Quinn and one of the other players on the front page."

Elation turned to realism of what work still had to be done when they were beaten by two points in the subsequent semi-final on home turf by their regular nemesis, Roscommon, then under the tutelage of former great, Dermot Earley. John immediately turned that negative into a positive, impressing on his players that the victory over Galway was an illustration of the ability within the side. The confidence, although shaken, remained intact. Hints of turning a considerable corner came at the end of an unspectacular 1993-1994 league campaign. Leitrim needed victory over Roscommon to ensure their place in Division Two while a defeat would mean a play-off game with the same opposition to decide who would go down. The stakes were obviously higher for Dermot Earley's men who knew what fate awaited if they lost.

"We didn't have a huge league but it came down to the game against Roscommon. We won that and consigned them to Division Three but it wasn't a case of consigning them to relegation. It was a significant victory, as the previous year Roscommon had beaten us in the championship and the league win was a nice connection point to the championship training. It gave us a great boost because we were paired with them in the first round of the Connacht championship that year."

Bellies were full of fire ahead of that game in Dr. Hyde Park and despite the baggage of suffering four consecutive championship defeats at the hands of their near neighbours, they rolled up the sleeves and put in a workmanlike display. In what turned out to be a game of two halves, Declan Darcy, whose frees were to prove crucial in that breakthrough year, converted the winner deep into injury-time.

The anticipation among the Leitrim faithful going into the semi-final joust against Galway was unprecedented. So much so, that the supporters were more nervous than the players themselves. "We played Galway in a terrible match in Carrick-on-Shannon. I'll never forget it - there was a full house and it was the one time in a match where I could hear myself shouting instructions. Our crowd were so nervous, they couldn't get behind the team. There was almost complete silence because there were very few from Galway there, it was nearly all Leitrim. Near the end, we won a free after Padraig McLoughlin, who had been only on a few minutes, had been fouled. Declan Darcy put over a long-range free to force a replay."

Tuam again proved a happy hunting ground in the replay. Leitrim turned around an eight points to six deficit at half-time and Padraig Kenny's point on the stroke of full-time, proved the winner, putting them into a Connacht final for the first time in twenty seven years. "The second half of that game was a highlight. I think Gary Fahy got injured and a few of our forwards, Colin McGlynn, Padraig Kenny and others, got some great scores. Winning two years in a row in Tuam was great for them at that stage. Then it was down to the Connacht final against Mayo in Hyde Park."

Leitrim were not only up against the defending champions of the previous two years but John was facing the ambiguous novelty of being up against his native county for the very first time. The professionalism he always brought to bear on his work served to hide personal feelings. "There would have been a bit of that, the fact that I was managing another team against my native county, but I would have said you have to divorce yourself from it. It was a traumatic time but it had to be a tunnel vision job. The thing to remember was that I felt nothing but goodwill, even when I took the Leitrim job. I found that there was nothing but goodwill from Mayo."

Conceding a goal after only eighteen seconds and a bad start in general sparked off familiar fears but this Leitrim side, thriving on composure and self-belief, manufactured a seven point lead going into the last quarter. Mayo's desperate onslaught that followed reduced the margin to a nail-biting two points in the closing stages but O'Mahony's defence were unyielding and the Nestor Cup returned to lovely Leitrim after an incredible absence of sixty seven years. Recalling those memories, it was clear that they were as vivid as if that triumphant achievement had happened yesterday. "The emotion of it all...the fact that the Mayo fans stayed on the field along with Leitrim people...there was huge goodwill."

His joy of being part of a historic day was as undiluted as the heaving mass of green and yellow that swamped Dr. Hyde Park that day. But, in glorious hours such as these, he was just as delighted for people who had toiled for the cause over many barren years as for his own personal sense of achievement.

Togged out and rearing to go... The Galway squad pictured at Croke Park prior to the All-Ireland final against Kildare. Back Row L to R: Brian Silke, Fergal Gavin, Padraic Boyce, Padraic Joyce, Tomás Meehan, Shay Walsh, Jarlath Fallon, Kevin Walsh, Seán Ó Domhnaill, Gary Fahy, John Divilly, Kevin Terry McDonncha, Tommy Joyce, Pat Comer, Michael Cloherty, Damien Mitchell. Front Row L to R: Paul Clancy, Robin Doyle, Micheál Geoghegan, Seán Óg de Paor, Michael Donnellan, Ray Silke, Derek Savage, Martin McNamara, Niall Finnegan, Tomás Mannion, Kevin Fallon, Tommie Wilson, Richie Fahy, Declan Meehan.

'Thirty two years of hurt never stopped us dreaming'... Galway captain Ray Silke holds the Sam Maguire triumphantly aloft.

Eyes down in Tuam... Niall Finnegan, Galway's last minute free-taking saviour, and Roscommon's Enon Gavin race for possession in the drawn Connacht final.

A picture of concentration... Derek Savage thinks about his next move during the Tuam tester.

Seeking support... Under pressure from Roscommon's Damien Donlon, Padraic Joyce opts to play possession back in the direction of his half-forward colleagues.

There she goes... Jarlath Fallon lets fly for a left-footed point in the Hyde Park Connacht final replay despite the outstretched attention of Roscommon captain, Clifford McDonald.

Left : Sweet smell of success... After 150 minutes of helter-skelter activity against Roscommon, Ray Silke finally gets his chance to hoist the Nestor Cup.

Below : 'You beauty'... An All-Ireland semi-final victory over Derry sealed, John O'Mahony receives hearty congratulations from a delighted Mick Byrne (left) and a magnanimous Derry manager, Brian Mullins.

'Sign, please'... Admiring fans queue up for Ray Silke's autograph during the build-up to the All-Ireland final.

Twin peaks... Seán Ó Domhnaill and Kevin Walsh, towering figures for Galway all season, stretch out at training in Tuam before the big game against Kildare.

Three wise men... Selectors Pete Warren and Stephen Joyce chew the fat with John O'Mahony during the Tuam press night ahead of the final.

'To Win Just Once'... Two of Tuam's favourite sons, Davy Carton and Leo Moran of The Sawdoctors, check out the feelings of another favourite son, Jarlath Fallon, in the lead-up to the Croke Park adventure.

The Medal Man... Mattie McDonagh, Connacht's most medal-laden Gaelic footballer, displays the four All-Ireland medals he won with Galway in 1956, 1964, 1965 and 1966.

Hail the three-in-a-row... The 1966 squad pictured prior to their victory at Croke Park against Meath. Back Row L to R: Seamus Leydon, Noel Tierney, Mick Reynolds, Mattie McDonagh, Sean Meade, Liam Sammon, John Keenan, Frank McLoughlin, Tom Sands, John 'Bosco' McDermott. Front Row L to R: Sean Cleary, Colie McDonagh, Cyril Dunne, Martin Newell, Enda Colleran, Jimmy Duggan, Pat Donnellan, John Donnellan, Christy Tyrrell, Johnny Geraghty.

Up for the final... Galway supporters, pictured en route to Croke Park and outside the Burlington hotel (bottom), soak up the atmosphere of final day in Dublin after a fifteen year absence.

Three steps to heaven... The moment Galway's grip on Sam Maguire strengthened irrevocably. First, Padraic Joyce skips clear of Kildare's John Finn. He then solos briefly before finally side-stepping the outfoxed goalkeeper, Christy Byrne, and powering home the crucial goal.

'Come back here'... Gary Fahy attempts to regain the ground lost to Kildare's Karl O' Dwyer who stoops to gather possession.

'Sting Ray'... Kildare's Willie McCreery gets no respite from Ray Silke while on the ball in Croke Park. Martin Lynch and Tomás Mannion monitor the tussle.

'Young gun having some fun'... Michael Donnellan, RTÉ's All-Ireland final man of the match, gathers possession in defence once more and readies himself to motor upfield despite Dermot Earley's approaching presence.

The Comeback Kid scales the heights... Martin McNamara, rounding off an unbelievable year of club and county All-Ireland success, gets shouldered aloft by some of his Corofin colleagues during the scenes of joy that followed referee John Bannon's final whistle against Kildare.

Arms aloft... Corner-back Tomás Meehan, with the new Cusack Stand providing the backdrop, is carried by a swaying human mass towards the Cusack Stand for the presentation of the Sam Maguire.

At work... John O'Mahony, crowning a remarkable first year in charge of Galway, enjoys his turn to clutch the Sam Maguire on the Hogan Stand podium following the defeat of Kildare.

At play... Back home in his native Ballaghaderreen on the Tuesday night after the final, the managerial marvel basks in the success with his family, daughters Niamh, Rhona, Deidre and Cliodhna and wife Gerardine. Missing from the photo is John's eldest daughter, Gráinne.

Bridging the Long Gap... Ray Silke and John O'Mahony poignantly carry the Sam Maguire into Connacht across the Old Town Bridge in Athlone, a symbolic moment that ended the thirty two year long wait for All-Ireland success in the province.

"I felt very much a Leitrim person that day. There was a great sense of satisfaction for the guys I had with me, Ollie Honeyman and Joe Reynolds. I was thrilled for them. These were two guys who had passionately been involved with Leitrim for so long. Reynolds had won an U-21 Connacht title in '77. Ollie Honeyman, for me, was the Willie Joe of Leitrim. I enjoyed working with them and they were brilliant. It was also fantastic for Tommie Moran, Tony McGowan, Eamon Tubman, Frank Darcy (father of Declan, trainer of the Dublin-based players) and all the other people who were constantly preaching Leitrim football down through the years."

The buzz of that success grew in ever bigger proportions considering their All-Ireland semi-final adventure pitted them against a Dublin side who at the time were being continually touted as All-Ireland material. It was an exciting prospect, rural minnows against city slickers. Right out of the David and Goliath mould. John was well aware of the marvellous backdrop but his objective was to try and win the game. The players adopted the same focus but, despite an unforgettable day at G.A.A. headquarters, Dublin had little time for sentiment. "Leitrim supporters were excited going into this big game against Dublin but I wanted to avoid the sense of occasion and win the match. We roared into the game and got the early start but the twelve point defeat was kind of a crunch. I was hurting for Leitrim in the sense that there was a big margin in it at the end. " Leitrim's fairytale had been met with a sucker-punch but this still did not stop supporters savouring a day that will live long in the memory. "I met people in the Burlington hotel that night who said I've got pictures I'm going to frame, pictures of Declan Darcy and stuff like that. I remember one saying that he was going to frame a picture of the scoreboard when Leitrim were leading Dublin by two points to one."

Victory in the 1994 Connacht final ended a truly wonderful year for Leitrim football. Not only had they possession of the Nestor Cup, they also had the proud statistic of losing just two competitive games out of eight. The exhaustive work, however, in reaping that success soon begin to exact a toll. A heavy defeat to Dublin, painful though it was, took a back seat compared to the failure to retain the provincial title in 1995. 'Bosco' McDermott's Galway, off the back of two tough games against Sligo, finally got the measure of Leitrim and took the title back to the coastal county after an eight year absence. Leitrim dominated much of the game but after Jarlath Fallon and Seán Óg de Paor levelled proceedings in the closing stages, their colleague Niall Finnegan converted the winning free in injury-time.

"If I had any regrets with Leitrim, it would have been that we did not get back to win in 1995 when Galway, fair play to them, caught us in the last few minutes down in Carrick. Leitrim were very unlucky in '95 and I know for a fact that if they had got back into Croke Park that year, it wouldn't have been a twelve point defeat. We would have given Tyrone a great shake, I really believe that. We had a few additions and we had learned from the experiences of '94."

As he spoke about that Leitrim-Galway game, it seemed a little peculiar that John mentioned players that he was now working with. Even then as Leitrim manager, he was acutely aware of the potential within Galway football. "We were leading going into full-time. I think Jarlath Fallon got a point to level it and Niall Finnegan got a free to win it. From the Galway perspective now, I got a lot of slagging - these guys came from the dead and went on to win a Connacht title. It showed the talent Galway had once they got going. I was very disappointed losing to them because I saw another chance of winning a Connacht title and Galway went on to hammer Mayo in the final. Even in those years when we would have beaten them, Galway were an exceptional team."

The scale of Leitrim's preparations involved huge demands from players, mentors and officials and, understandably, the defeat punched a few holes in the enthusiasm that coursed through the team in those seasons. Leitrim's heavy workload was more pronounced considering that there was a large geographical diaspora of players. After "holding their own" in the 1995-1996 league, Leitrim were again pitted against the Tribesmen. It was a game that saw Declan Darcy deployed in the forward-line for the first time ever in the championship. And it is also remembered for an excellent top corner strike from the Leitrim captain. That score, coming in injury-time, came near the tail-end of a remarkable Leitrim revival. Within the space of six minutes, an eight point margin was finally whittled down to a point before Finnegan, who was in scintillating form, put over the last of his five scores from play to seal the issue.

It was an enthralling finish but, in truth, Galway, controlling the exchanges until those frantic last moments, were deserving winners. The casing around the Leitrim dream bubble was now finally beginning to crack. "After '95 and '96, it was difficult to come back. The Leitrim thing was exceptionally hard and demanding for the players. They were scattered and winning a Connacht final for them was like winning an All-Ireland. You would be trying to freshen up the team and bring in new players. I would be saying to them that they would have to do things better than anyone else but to do that with the geographical spread we had was difficult."

Before that game, John had made his mind up to depart the scene after Leitrim's interest in the 1996 championship had ended. Ironically, it was Tuam, a venue that previously held a lot of good memories for him as

Leitrim manager, which brought the curtains down on a memorable adventure. The feelings in a hushed dressing-room afterwards were understandably poignant. "It was the end of an adventure. The feelings were very personal and I'll never forget it. There was great respect between me and the players and I didn't want to get emotional. I remember the disappointment, I said a few words and they just stood up and clapped."

Similar to his involvement with Mayo, the many friendships he developed over that time are still very fresh, something that he treasures deeply. And those special ties were very evident in the run up to this year's All-Ireland final. "I made an awful lot of friends during my time with Leitrim. I would say out of a panel of twenty five players, twenty players contacted me before the All-Ireland either by phone or card. Nothing can compensate for that. Fellas I would have worked extremely hard with, that's what sport is all about." The regrets on leaving were inevitable but John was clear in his mind about the decision. "I enjoyed it and felt I had done a reasonable job. I would have said to myself 'I enjoyed it, I'm going to miss it' but it was absolutely the right decision that I took."

Running through those thoughts is a fundamental part of a philosophy that continues to give him the sobering perspective he needs to carry out his work as effectively as possible. "It also shows that you don't own Leitrim. The football in any county is always going to be bigger. You become a central figure for a period of time and it's important that if you are a central figure, you realise you are not bigger that the whole football issue itself. The thing is bigger."

His earthy perspective has also provided a cushion for any criticism that is always at some stage part and parcel of team management. John has been luckier than many, considering his achievements with Mayo, Leitrim and Galway. But like all managers, no matter how successful, criticism is an inevitable part of sport. John acknowledges that being under the microscope jibes are inescapable, but looking at the nature of managing a successful team he also warns of the dangers involved when at the top in any sport.

"Criticism hurts me, it has always hurt me. But the longer you're in this, the less hurt there will be. Maybe in earlier years you would have reacted to criticism but it is the opinion of one person. I would say that to the players as well. In a lot of cases, people are entitled to their opinions as long as it doesn't get personal, especially when you consider they're amateur players. There'll be ups and downs in any one's career but there's more downs and ups though. I suppose when you've done something special, that's when you're on a high and you kind of say that this is great but don't start believing in it too much." It is a viewpoint that he tries to impress upon the players he has worked with. "If you ask me how I've developed as a manager, that's one of the things that I'd been trying to get across to the players. They're everybody's favourite now but it's important for them to retain a sense of perspective."

By the end of his four-year Leitrim stint, John O'Mahony had now earned a reputation as being one of the most astute managers in the country. It is an accepted fact that his preparations are meticulous, measured and very personalised when it comes to dealing with players. It was after Mayo's All-Ireland final appearance in 1989 that the rumour mill concerning John O'Mahony's approach first began to stir itself into action. Word of a sports psychologist being employed back then to induce self-belief is common currency along the highways and byways. What were the magic ingredients he used for maximising the talent at his disposal, many people wondered. The elixir, whatever it was, had reaped highly successful dividends.

The rumour mongering was, in effect, the beginning of a quest by the public and, gradually, the media to seek insights into his training methods. It wasn't so much the physical training that intrigued - most top county team's physical preparations do not vary that much today - but the manner in which his mental tunings could turn dormant potential into winning talent. All too aware of the publicity surrounding his involvement with teams, understandably any queries into the techniques employed by John are met with a protective response. Many of his thoughts appear to be vetted solely out of trust and loyalty for the backroom team and an exclusive set of other people who combine to make up that important inner circle.

"Over the years, we'd prepare teams well and pride ourselves on being ahead of the posse in certain things we did. We prepared our teams well but there are certain parts of my management where I don't know want to name the people involved. There are many areas where I get experts in, whether it be management, medical or whatever, but in a hundred years time when somebody says who was involved with Galway at the time, my name will be there but there will be names of people that won't be there."

What he does reveal is that there has been a solid continuity in his preparations over the years. The approach has effectively been the same since his days with Mayo. In that time, there have been, and still are, a number of people very close to him whose identity will always remain a closely guarded secret. They continue to play an important part in the development of John O'Mahony as a highly regarded team manager.

His need to maintain that seal of confidentiality has led inevitably to much speculation as to the other more enigmatic people. "There would be a lot of continuity in what I have done but sometimes mis-information comes out as did some of the things that came out after this year's All-Ireland as to 'who did what' or whatever. As regards the mental preparation, some of the stuff that came out after this year's All-Ireland, particularly the week after, was way off-beam. There were some things said about our minute preparation and they were very wide of the mark. What I'm trying to get across is that it's better to keep all these things private, there's no need for anyone to know really. The magic formula is this: loyalty and trust between me and my friends. Including the players, I'd say there would be fifty people, maybe less than that who are involved. For me, it has been direct involvement, for others, it would have been peripheral and if I name forty five of them and leave out the five, then that's hurtful to the five I leave out. These people know that I'm thanking them globally. That's why I deflect attention because it's not my victory. People will say that 'x' and 'y' did that but as far as I'm concerned, there are things done that no-one will ever know about. All I will say about preparations of any of the teams I'm involved with is that I feel that they have been the best prepared teams, better than any professional sports team.

"You pick up bits and pieces about how teams prepare, and that would include looking at other sports. It's the same thing that's involved. When you're into that kind of thing, you are always looking at how you do this and that...you're always learning." The whole idea of meticulous and expert preparation is a gospel that he also uses to motivate the players. "Even when I use the language to the players, I would say to them that 'ye prepared better than anyone else'. I really am trying to get across that point. It's not a mystique. It's loyalty to a group rather than me being all of that group."

In articulating his thoughts on the achievements and the successes he has been central to, he defines his role as a co-ordinator - picking what he sees as the best people for the job and ensuring that the subsequent mix blends properly.

It became a proven recipe that reaped the ultimate reward two years later.

7

Scaling The Summit

"It was a big honour and it was the first time Galway had gone outside for a manager. It was a new challenge for me going from the Leitrim set-up because here you were going to a county with a lot of player resources and a lot of under-age talent. There was also the obvious sense of excitement."

After the Leitrim adventure, the next chapter in the management career of John O'Mahony could not have been more different to the one he had left behind. Maximising scant playing resources was the challenge in his previous position, while the considerable task of finding the right blend among what seemed a luxury of young talent appeared the job description in Galway.

Football in Galway in 1995 was making substantial but still tentative steps away from the barren years that blighted the county for almost a decade. A Connacht title that year, under the stewardship of 'Bosco' McDermott, was followed by a rousing and enlightening display against a strong Tyrone side in the All-Ireland semi-final. Galway did reach another Connacht final in 1996 but a resurgent Mayo side presented too many questions that were not answered. Division Three remained the stomping ground in the 1996-1997 season before new player-manager Val Daly had his charges overthrown in a Tuam thriller later that summer at the hands of Mayo, All-Ireland finalists of the previous year. Daly's first taste of inter-county management thus met a premature and controversial end after just one season.

John O'Mahony's name flashed and wailed like a siren at the top of many recommendation lists among Galway clubs in the aftermath, and it was inevitable that the job would be laid at his door. He was honoured by the interest shown and after eventually accepting the position, the work immediately began to assess a somewhat jumbled picture.

The scale of the exercise may have been similar to the Mayo job back in 1987 but the angle of the approach was much different for this set of players. A number of those illustrated the rich under-age talent that had come off the conveyor-belt. That assembly line had produced five U-21 and four minor provincial titles since 1990. Young guns, Michael Donnellan and Tomás Meehan had made their initial forays into senior waters in the previous championship and along with the 1998 debutantes, Padraic Joyce, John Divilly, Derek Savage and Richie Fahy (brother of full-back, Gary), it was clear that there was plenty of young jewels, albeit unpolished, at John's disposal. "Back in '87, I was taking over a Mayo team that had been around for a few years and was high up on the development curve. This Galway team was one that was young and the average age was twenty three or twenty four. They did have some older players and the challenge of course was to blend the two. I was excited by the fact that there was a better chance to get ideas through to a younger group like that."

Taking on a job that was dripping with so much tradition was intimidating enough but added to the mix was that much of the resources available, while extremely promising, still needed plenty of guidance and co-ordination. The magnitude of the work soon became clear after he assumed office last September. "You're starting out like a builder coming on to a new building site. You're building it from the foundations again. Part of the situation coming in was to pick my own selectors and I had to literally start from scratch and a put a team around me."

With players on holidays and others involved in club championships, plus the fact that Galway had been knocked out the previous May, the jigsaw in those early stages was well scattered. Players like Jarlath Fallon and Tomás Mannion had committed themselves to rugby (neither player joined the panel until spring), Niall Finnegan was not due to return until after Christmas and John Divilly, a U.C.D. student, did not become a central figure until the New Year. Consequently, John's selectors, Stephen Joyce and Pete Warren, two fiercely proud Galway men, became his crucial reference points. The decision to have them on board was well thought out.

"Stephen was somebody who had done it all with Galway. He had played in an All-Ireland final and had won five Connacht championship medals. He also won a national league medal and is still playing a bit of club football, so he was very much in the know. Pete Warren would also have played for Galway over a shorter term and had the advantage of coaching Tuam to a Connacht club title in 1994, so I would be very conscious of the fact that they had the finger very much on the pulse of Galway football. Not that I meant to do it that way but they were also located geographically on different sides of the county. I felt it would be tying the thing together nicely. I wouldn't have known them personally beforehand. I would have known Stephen before and I would have known Pete from a distance, but once I got to know them well I realised they were good choices."

Set against the backdrop of his first few weeks in the new job was Mayo's second All-Ireland title bid, something that was used as an early motivational device. "On September 13th, we had our first trial game and in the training sessions that followed, it would have come across to me that our lads were very conscious of the fact that Mayo were preparing for an All-Ireland. I was also conscious that there was a great respect and a great support, and a hope that they would win it. It would have been a benefit to our preparations and an incentive in the sense that Galway had run Mayo so close last year and that incentive was there to work even harder. It gave them a marker that at least the team that beat them was up there." Aside from the obvious goal of making an impact in the championship, the immediate objective was to achieve Division One status. "Basically, what was in our minds was to win league games but project ourselves to a long-term plan so that we could fill in the jigsaw."

Galway were a Division Three side when John stepped in but with the league restructure at the beginning of last season, it appeared at the time that those finishing top of their restructured groups would secure places in the higher divisions the following year. A wry smile creases John's lips when he recalls the night he was informed of their particular league grouping. "We phoned Croke Park and found out who we were playing. I laughed when I heard it. Leitrim first and Mayo second and I said 'who planned this?'.

Ironically, getting off to a good start as Leitrim manager five years previously went full circle in October 1997 when he chalked up his first win as Galway manager against his near neighbours. At the beginning of November, the early rollercoaster reached the top of the curve in the following game with a foretaster of the summer clash against Mayo. Pulling a crowd of ten thousand to McHale Park, the game vibrated with championship-like fervour. Mayo pulled the strings for much of the exchanges and it took a late Shay Walsh point to ensure a share of the spoils. "I enjoyed the day to some extent but I was also conscious of the fact that people were going to read a lot more into than was actually there. I mean if Mayo won or Galway won, what would it have proved at the end of the day?. In many ways it was the best result possible as it left the situation open to next May."

Galway drew with Laois at Ballinasloe in their third league game and John felt that the remaining game against Louth before the winter break needed to be won in order to stay in the top half of the table. It would also be a measure of the progress to date against their opponents who were coming into the game off the back of seven successive wins, including an All-Ireland 'B' success. In an extremely impressive display, Galway chalked up a 1-12 to 1-9 victory in Drogheda and commentators at the time observed a notable poise and swagger developing. John was pleased at the response from his players. "It was a huge one to win and we put as much as possible into winning in the wintertime situation. I remember we had a few injury problems going into that. Niall Finnegan had not been playing with us. He got married and was to rejoin us after Christmas but I remember getting on to him to come in for a few training sessions and we put him on the bench against Louth that day. It was hugely important that he rallied for that particular game and he epitomised the spirit. He had been taking his break but when he saw the emergency, he came in."

The win put them in a strong position to secure a quarter-final place and that materialised when remaining games in the New Year turned out to be facile affairs against Fermanagh, Carlow and Kilkenny. The Corofin contingent, involved in what turned out to be a historic All-Ireland club campaign, were missing for those games but John was happy that the squad and team unit were getting stronger. Inevitably, there was still tinkering to be done in defence and midfield, which had an unsettled look during the league, but there was plenty of confidence ahead of the quarter-final tie against Offaly in Dr. Hyde Park last April. It turned out to be a rather forgettable day on many fronts, however, when a composed Offaly, winning by four points, deservedly progressed at the expense of a fitful Galway. John, as always, concentrated on the positives ahead of the championship game at the end of May.

"The weather was terrible that day and we clocked up fourteen wides. Offaly got a goal from a break and we missed a goal opportunity. I would have been disappointed with the result but there were a lot of things that I felt were o.k., you know. It helped everyone re-focus their minds on what needed to be done for the championship. The fact that we got to the quarter-final of the league meant that there was no break between training. There was not much time to get back on course. Again, it was shoulders to the wheel stuff in training and it really showed the level of commitment from the players. So we met on the Tuesday night after the league match and Jarlath Fallon joined then. So it went from there."

The preparations for the championship became intense in all respects. Training soon took on a precision-like feel. No stone was left unturned. "Preparing for the championship, you have to get physically and mentally right. That preparation is intense for the players firstly but particularly intense for the management. Every player is as important as the next and you have to try and get around to everyone to see how they're feeling, what their aims are or what they need to improve on. Training is serious but people have also got to enjoy it. You've got to make sure that the objectives of what you have set out are still there when you're coming away from sessions." For John and his selectors, picking the right stuff for the final fifteen was always going to be difficult.

"You'd be driving back from training and you'd be picking the team in your mind. You'd be seeing how it was coming together and how the injury situation was and stuff like that. Picking a championship team is a soul-searching exercise, taking into account the players you leave out and it is one of the most gut-wrenching things a management team has to do." Team selection, in view of its importance to the harmony within a squad, understandably is a thorough process. "We'd pick a team, come back, sleep on it and come back and meet again. Sometimes, certain positions are so tight, we might even change something. If the spirit is good enough in the group, there will be no problem with team selections. But if you have a bad spirit in the team, if the thing is not right, you're going to have a lot of bitching. What pleased me this year was that there were a lot of hard decisions when the team was picked for the Mayo game. There were a lot of close calls. But when you tell a guy that he is not in the team and he says 'I'm ready if you need me', then you get a good feeling for the match that Sunday."

The noisy cauldron of McHale Park in that first round game was the litmus test for a Galway team under a manager with a hot reputation. An excellent start from the visitors preceded a second quarter that was brimming with entertainment and one which left the sides level at the break (2-5 to 1-8) after contributing some fabulous scores. It was a period when Derek Savage pulled the trigger for a wonderful goal but one in which Mayo had also plundered two, the products of some slack marking.

Loose defending, not suprisingly, was top of the agenda at the break. "From a neutral point of view, the first half was a fantastic spectacle. From our point of view and from Mayo's point of view, we wouldn't be happy with it. It was positive football, there was no negativity but we knew we had a lot of work to do in the second half. They got two goals and they could have got two more, so I knew we had to tighten down the hatches considerably.

That instruction was carried out perfectly. "The predominant thought from that game would have been the second half. I thought we had battened down the hatches even though we weren't scoring as freely. Our style of play after half-time and the way we closed the game down is the prominent thought. It wasn't until the later stages that our dominance was reflected on the scoreboard. Derek Savage's goal was another highlight. It was great to see that go in because in our lead-up and challenge games, we did not score a huge amount of goals." The shudder of a crossbar after Kieran McDonald, Mayo's best forward, unleashed a vicious strike late in the game is still a sobering memory, however. "That shot that came off the crossbar - you wouldn't be here talking to me now if that had gone in. There were anxious moments but that was the only time that that kind of looseness was there in the second half."

Many talking points peppered the post-mortems but one of the liveliest was the deployment at centre-back of one of the three debutantes, John Divilly, a move precipitated by Robin Doyle not having recovered from injury. The re-alignment saw captain Ray Silke move from the middle of defence to the wing and Tomás Mannion revert to corner-back. It was a defensive formation that remained unchanged for the rest of the championship.

Designating a free role to Divilly was the tactic that paid the richest dividend on that warm day. Along with neutralising Mayo's stamina-man, Colm McMenamon, Divilly's long, direct deliveries were lapped-up by Galway's on-song forward-line. "In the lead-up to the first round in the championship, you're always going to have a situation where you won't know exactly what the opposition is doing and you won't make it easier for them in terms of what you're doing either. John Divilly actually had an injury situation as well as Robin Doyle and we weren't sure if he'd come through. When you win, you can always say tactically it worked. Tactically, sometimes it works and sometimes it doesn't. When you win a championship game like that, there is an enthusiasm to work on these things. That game had dominated our winter, our thoughts and everything."

Another talking point among pundits concerned some creaky defending by the winners. "Maybe the perception was created then that our defence was weak, that it was there for the taking. It was a perception which wasn't killed but maybe it was no bad thing that that perception was there. It gave us an opportunity to work on it and make sure that we were able to refine that."

Amid all the hoopla that day among the Galway faithful, however, John was aware that he had pricked the Mayo bubble of the previous two years. "I was also very conscious of the fact that it was a kind of death knell for Mayo in context of the high they had been on. I knew that experience in '89-90. It was only for a year at that stage but when you see Mayo on a rollercoaster and having played in three All-Irelands...again I wasn't doing it in a sniding way. I did genuinely feel sorry to have nipped them in the bud in that sense."

Up next was the familiar sight of Leitrim. Galway's last visit to the Carrick-on-Shannon venue three seasons previous had proved productive in a highly competitive affair. Much was expected this time around but it proved a hugely one-sided game. "We were expecting a tough challenge but it turned out totally different. I was surprised at the result because I know those Leitrim players were better than they showed that day. I was expecting a dogged battle. Leitrim played Mayo in the league, I wasn't at it but people who were said that Mayo were awfully lucky to win it. Apart from the fact that I would have known Leitrim myself, the one thing is they might not win a huge amount, but they certainly make it tough for anyone who plays them. That was the tradition I tapped into when I was there.

"We won very well but I felt a little bit for Leitrim to be honest. At that stage, I was treading on a lot of egg-shells after Mayo and Leitrim and it was a draining time for me. Coming from that Leitrim game, I met a couple of their players going to the hotel. I had spoken to the Leitrim team in their dressing-room after the game but this was on a personal level and I must say that they were very, very gracious."

Despite the victory, features such as shooting and concentration were designated as prime areas for improvement. The other worry was that the expectations hovering around Galway increased significantly. "There were areas that I would be saying that we need to pick up on, and that's what I was coming away with whereas supporters were coming away with the idea that there was no point taking Roscommon seriously. And that created a difficult situation for the Connacht final." Galway were firm favourites to win their first Connacht title in three years at Tuam Stadium but John reveals candidly that their opponents were being treated very seriously within the camp. "I was apprehensive enough going into the Roscommon game. I knew we were on a hiding to nothing. I saw a huge improvement in Roscommon from the Sligo game the first day. I genuinely felt that and there was none of the crazy mistakes that were made in Hyde Park. There were two things I felt were important going into that match: Roscommon's improvement from game to game and the gap between our last game. There was also an unreality around our team in terms of expectation."

At a rain-soaked Tuam, Galway were given the fright of their lives by a tremendously spirited and physically-strong Roscommon team, galvanised by Jason Neary's sudden dismissal in the last quarter. That fright extended itself to the final minute when Niall Finnegan was forced to knock over a nail-biting free to force a replay. "People would have said after the game that the bad weather affected our game but this is one of the things I would be saying to teams 'if you want to make excuses, you'll find them'. It wasn't really the weather. Our attitude wasn't as good as it should have been and the reason why we played poorly was that we allowed Roscommon to come back and run at us in the second half. In the last twenty minutes of that game, we were terrible. I was worried of course. We had the extra-man, we were winning the kick-outs short but Roscommon were coming back at us in waves.

"The decision to use the short kick-out worked but we were slow to get the ball forward. We did the same thing with the short kick-outs against Derry when we had an extra man but we got the ball forward more quickly in that game. It was a scary last twenty minutes, but even when Roscommon went in front in the last few minutes we always felt we could get back. People also talk about Gary Fahy's supposed pick off the ground before Niall Finnegan's free but should Michael Donnellan have been pulled for that hand-pass in the second half? He was penalised for that but if you were getting a coaching video on how to hand-pass a ball correctly, you could have used it as an example. Only for being penalised on that, we would have been been out sight as it would have put us three points ahead. Those things balance out. I would have also thought Gary Fahy didn't pick the ball off the ground but wouldn't I think that?. Even if it was off the ground, there would have been decisions either way over the course of that game."

"In fairness to Roscommon, I thought if we had stolen it, it would have been a steal. I was impressed with them. There were fine examples of teamwork and fine examples of young players coming of age on the Roscommon side. I was pleased to get a replay and pleased to get another chance. I would have loved to have gone into that game the way our opponents went into it. I was pleased we had come through that game at Tuam as we had been made raging hot favourites. It was a huge lesson to our players. The lads felt that they didn't just perform and they wanted to get it right. There was a huge emphasis on the second day and we had a fortnight to do that."

The replay in an atmospheric Dr. Hyde Park in front of a large and partisan home crowd continued where the drawn game had left off. It was tense and tight but Roscommon went two points in front with about ten minutes to go. Galway responded in style, playing their best football and forging a one point lead with two minutes left on the clock. "When Roscommon went ten points to eight up, that was a defining moment for me in that game. It was either 'our guys respond to this or not' and I had a good feeling that they would and it was great to see it happening on the field. There were a few balls that had to be won and they were won. If we were a team of little character, the heads would have gone down at that stage, the tent would have folded and Roscommon might have gone on to win by five or six points. There was something there deep down and it was great to see it unfolding from a Galway point of view. I felt after that we should have won it in normal time. I felt when we went eleven-ten clear we were going to win it until Eddie Lohan's free interceded. We had a lot of bad wides against Leitrim and in the drawn game against Roscommon. But I always felt that we had the forwards to take their chances and if they were creating them, it wasn't a terminal illness."

With the momentum going into extra-time, Galway manufactured a significant two point lead in the first period of extra-time. The decisive turning point came minutes after the restart when a goalkeeping error helped provide the platform for victory. "Ja Fallon hit the ball in and it was a shot that should have been a point but it dropped short. What pleased me was that we had the players on hand to take advantage of Derek Thompson's slip. They put on pressure without fouling, which is what you're looking for - it's very easy to foul a goalie. The ball went away from him, Michael Donnellan got the touch and it was great to see it going in. It was the cushion we were looking for."

Galway closed the game out with an impressive level of fitness and John was additionally pleased that the team would not have to experience another long waiting game as the All-Ireland semi-final was only three weeks away. The wides quota again figured high in the Connacht final replay match coverage but John prefers to see it as a team having the ability to generate those chances. "I wouldn't have seen it as a concern. I would have seen it in terms of an incentive to improve on. If we had twenty wides and scored 1-17, even if we got fifty per cent of the wides, we would have scored about 1-27. It would have put us out of sight of Roscommon and then made us overwhelming favourites against Derry. Now, I had a good idea that we weren't going to have twenty wides against Derry. The bottom line is that I always knew that our forwards were good enough to take chances and I said it at the time that I would give huge credit to the Roscommon defence which put a lot of pressure on our forward-line. There was a lot of relief after that game and part of it was that we had done what we had set out to do. I also felt, in a funny kind of way, we had got to a situation where a team was going into an All-Ireland campaign on the backfoot."

John believes that the Roscommon games were of huge benefit and probably the making of his team which had to dig deep a number of times in two-and-a-half hours of gruelling football. Stretched minds and weary limbs there may have been but thoughts quickly had to turn to the All-Ireland semi-final joust against Derry. Two of the three weeks before that game were devoted to ball skills and fine-tuning the fitness and stamina levels, while sandwiched in between was a week of intense training. Everything was now geared for an encounter against a less than assured Derry side that had squeezed out of Ulster.

Brian Mullen's charges had booked their passage to the penultimate stage in rather unconvincing fashion but John feels that the Northern team were still guaranteed plenty of media coverage. It was just what he wanted. "I would have seen Derry as a team with a high profile and high profile people that had done it all, so to speak. They still had a fair bit to prove going into the semi-final. People close to football would have known that but the general perception was they were a team yearning for a breakthrough since '93. They were well used to playing big games in Croke Park so there was a fear that they would come good as well."

Producing the goods on the big stage was the solid faith John placed in his players. Such was the confidence that you could almost accuse his words of betraying caution. "I was confident we would play well in Croke Park. We had come out of Connacht after a heavy expectation and I knew the team was talented. There was still a lot of expectancy but I felt if we could express ourselves well, there was no reason why we could not win the game. We had a respect for Derry but there was no inferiority complex. I knew this Galway team were talented in terms of skill and character after that crucial stage in the second half of the Roscommon replay. I also knew they were talented in terms of commitment when I watched that unfold in Connacht."

Derry were mastered with control, composure and an impressive level of maturity. Galway always looked in command against a team who simply did not have the cutting edge to make any inroads. There was a desperate scramble by the Northern side at the finish but the Tribesmen's five point victory reflected an extremely professional display. Derry's robust style of tackling also played into his side's hands. "We got a great start and Padraic Joyce's free-taking got us some good early scores. The game was a justification for penalising consistent fouling. It was an indication of that and I suppose Derry, on the day, suffered perhaps from a lack of discipline. We benefited from the fact that we had a lot of possession, we ran at them and then they fouled us. We were ahead by six points at half-time and they came back at us but we got over that. At half-time we were keen that there was a job to be finished here. Derry came back at us in the second half but their short passing didn't help them on the day. The prominent memory for me was the strong finish we had. I also felt that we improved our accuracy. I was pleased that we had only three wides in that game." Again, the victory was hugely satisfying but the players retained that important sense of perspective. "There was a great sense of satisfaction but I was delighted to see that it was without a sense of euphoria. There's nothing for winning an All-Ireland semi-final and I know that more than most with my previous experiences."

Plenty of column inches were devoted to Galway and Kildare's head-to-head on September 27th. John, well-experienced in such matters, knew that the intense media publicity would never be too far away and it is a feature over the years he accepts - as long as it doesn't serve as a distraction. "I think as long as people know the parameters and when it doesn't interfere with preparations, then there's no problem. My feelings are and always have been that it is important that the sections of the media are allowed to do their job. It can be good for players and it can be good for their profiles as long as they realise it is not an end in itself. From a footballer's point of view, if they start believing this stuff, well..."

He also needs little prompting when he describes the beneficial effects the media can have for the game and its players. "If there wasn't live coverage, there would be fewer players who would want to play the game. Whether we like it or not, there is a buzz being involved and T.V. helps that high profile." High profile are words that describe the media coverage of Galway and, in particular, Kildare's lead-in to the big day. Vibrant colour bedecked both counties, excitement was reaching fever pitch and John had to make sure that to balance that atmosphere with the need to keep the players' minds uncluttered.

"It was a conscious thing to let the players enjoy the occasion but also to let them know what was in store for them and try and condition supporters to the fact that there was a serious job of work to be done. I would have to say though that the supporters were excellent. There was a sense of goodwill everywhere we went but there was no sense of hysteria that interfered with our preparations. We had a press night and I was pleased with the way it went. We trained the Tuesday and the Thursday the second week before the game and had the press night on the Wednesday."

With the media getting their fill, the following ten days were free of distraction. Here, John clarifies a notion doing the rounds back then that the final training sessions were closed off to the public. "There was no cut-off point. We sort of put out the word that if you wanted to go to a training session, there was a press night to come and see. That worked out fine but we didn't have any of our sessions behind closed doors at all." Preparations also involved a morale-building weekend trip for the squad.

"We had a weekend away and it was a case of time together. It gave us time to do a bit of tactical stuff and time for a few discussions. Preparations went smoothly."

John looks back with an almost tangible sense of appreciation that the squad, barring a calf injury to Kevin Walsh and Paul Clancy's broken foot, had remained injury free. That heavenly situation before him was even more remarkable considering that a full squad of players were chomping at the bit at training. "We had thirty fit players, we had two trial games in the weeks ahead of the All-Ireland and they were giving it everything in training. That was a great position to be in. All these players had done the same training programme and were gunning for places. There was a danger of injuries because you'd see full commitment. But luckily we had no injuries and we had a good medical team behind us. We were very lucky all year in the sense that the only major worry we had was Paul Clancy who broke a bone in his foot in the Leitrim game. It was a stress fracture. It had to be put into a cast and he missed out on the Connacht final and the All-Ireland semi-final. That again epitomised the commitment for me. Paul had no chance of playing in the Connacht final and All-Ireland semi-final but he was in the gym doing weights. He would go to training and do the laps and I was delighted for him that he got a run in the final."

Final day itself was a wonderful sea of maroon and white, with a heady atmosphere matching the feel-good factor coursing through the stands. Laois, having unsuccessfully bid for a third consecutive minor title earlier in the afternoon, lined up near the entrance to the old dressing rooms to applaud the winning Tyrone team that had experienced its share of tragedy in the last two years. It was a memorable cameo in a day of many special moments.

There were some surprises too, although most of them had been anticipated by Galway. The reshuffling of the Kildare line-out after the throw-in was the first challenge to John and his team. It was pretty much old news that the injury to full-back Ronan Quinn had ruled him out of the side, but did that surgery to the Lilywhites' formation cause any food for thought? "We were ready for anything. We had a fair idea of what the alternative was so we wouldn't be allowing anything to deflect us mentally from that. You feel sometimes that things like that turn against you. They lost Niall Buckley and they seemed to use that as a spur. It was no surprise though when John Finn went to full-back, as he had played there before."

Identical to all of their games, a good start was summoned by Galway, putting three points on the board. Then, for some unknown reason, the game-plan started to unravel at an alarming rate, quickened by a Dermot Early goal. "We got a good start and then had a sticky patch. It was a worrying period but it's very hard to say what happened. In tactical terms, we deliberated too much on the ball, we stopped running. When we had the ball, we weren't getting it forward and when we didn't have it, they were running at us and we were on the backfoot. What the actual mental process was, I don't know. I think Kildare's goal changed things. There was a period ten minutes from the break where we tried to get to grips with the game. It was only the minute or two before Padraic Joyce got that free near half-time that we starting winning possession.

"In hindsight now, what happened in the first half was even better because if we had continued as strong as we started, they would have had a chance to come back at us. I wasn't worried about Kildare in the first half, they are a good team, but it was very unlikely they were going to dominate for the seventy minutes. Then came the famous half-time interval."

Such was the dramatic turnaround in style and tempo of Galway's play immediately after the break that the words of wisdom imparted during the interval have almost become legendary at this stage. Not surprisingly, John takes the heat out of a burning sub-plot that dominated many of the Monday headlines. "A lot has been written about and speculated on what was said at half-time but it was fairly straightforward. A lot of things have been embellished a little bit and some of the reports about what went on at half-time are not right."

Hearsay and rumour also fed some of the media speculation surrounding Galway's preparations on the weekend of the All-Ireland final, according to John. He is quick to emphasise that much of it wasn't based on any degree of accuracy. "Again, in the euphoria of an All-Ireland victory, some things would have been recorded or reported on as regards what happened that weekend, at team meetings on Saturday night and at half-time on Sunday. Those things were way off the mark, a sort of poetic licence being taken by some journalists. Some of things that were supposed to have been said would be the last things that would be said and I want to put that on the record. As regards what was actually said at half-time - I said this around the week of the All-Ireland and I'll say it now - the tactical plan was hatched and had been talked about at length before we got to Dublin at all because, at that time, the absorption rate was not as great. So, it was a matter of getting back the messages of re-implementing that. Nothing more, nothing less."

So simple an explanation for such a dramatic transformation after the break, it almost sounds deceiving but John's emphasis on the game-plan throughout the year had already provided the methods coming into the game. It was now just a matter of divining those thoughts again from his players, reactivating the implanted microchip, if you like. "I was delighted with the way we responded after half-time. We got a crucial goal and that was a turning point. For me, what was more of a turning point was when I saw our game-plan back into action. It wasn't until Seán Óg put us four points ahead...that was the feeling...that was the point when we said 'we have it'. It was a great feeling. It brought a lot of things flooding out. Obviously from a calmness point of view, we still had a few balls to win. I had to make sure that they were picking people up, but in fairness the lads themselves were doing it and there was a great sense of finishing the job."

The sense of completion did not stop there. Paul Clancy's introduction in the latter stages ensured that the team which started out in May against Mayo was the side that finished the championship. "It was days after that when somebody reminded me of this. Paul Clancy came in for the last few minutes and it closed the chapter on a very successful campaign."

Echoes of 'The Fields of Athenry' sung in a sea of emotion after the game may be a little faded in the mind now but the reminders are still around every corner. Since that watershed September day, John, the mentors and the players have been sucked into a whirlpool of goodwill gushing from many counties. Endless invitations to functions and events, big and small, have flooded in the Galway door and not surprisingly, there is still a sense of dizziness about it all as I spoke to him a few short weeks before the start of the 1998-1999 national football league.

In the face of such revelry, John remains as philosophical and calm as ever, even though the fall-out from an All-Ireland title victory is unchartered territory for this young team. "It has been a rollercoaster since with the celebrations and stuff like that. We're within two weeks of the league as we sit here, and there's a sense of looking to the future. The challenge up to now has been to be successful, the challenge now is how to cope with the success. For my own part, I want to make the right decisions as regards the team and what my involvement will be. I want to be with them if they want to be successful. There is a lot of potential but that is the huge challenge that is before them."

For many of the players, another big test will be dealing with the new-found fame and its consequences. In a footballing context, they will become the team that everyone wants to beat. In a wider sense, such a momentous victory can be life-changing. "Winning an All-Ireland transforms people's lives in every sense. In the past few weeks there has been job offers for some of the fellas and the whole general area of demands has put a strain on their time. Really, what they have to realise is that when they won it, they had to work enormously hard. They're going to have to work twice as hard to retain it. Are they prepared to do that? It's easy to say 'yes' but it's another thing to act upon it."

Listening to John's cautious words gives a fair indication of his objective to ensure that the players fully enjoy the spoils of victory but also keep that all-important sense of perspective. Such a mindset should ensure the staying power of a team with the undoubted potential for many more memorable days.

Foundations for a squad with the maturity to deal with the pressures ahead already look firmly in place. For John and the players, family support has been pivotal in a year that needed those unbreakable structures in place. Sporting success depends on a network of families, wives, girlfriends and other miscellaneous links. "I couldn't have done what I've done without the support of my wife Gerardine and the kids, and the wider family circle as well, my own two brothers and also Ger's family. Sport, at the end of the day, is a fierce personal thing for the thirty people involved. Each of them have support and you know, I've seen players who have been made huge players because of that. People would say that I've transformed some of the older players but I know what has brought about the transformation - their families, their wives, some of them who are newly married. These people have made an immense difference."

There is still some unfinished business. First, the inevitable poser. How can these All-Ireland winners be viewed in the context of the three-in-a-row team? "I think there would be no-one gladder than the players of the sixties that Galway won this year. Secondly, no-one will be saying to our own players 'would ye like to be like them'. I suppose they will be saying that the sixties team won three-in-a-row but this year's All-Ireland win does get the monkey off the back for Galway and Connacht."

This leads nicely to the closing question and one which really doesn't need an answer: What has Galway's 1998 All-Ireland success done for Connacht? "Galway will be hoping that they will be there again but whoever gets to an All-Ireland or gets to an All-Ireland series from Connacht, I know it'll make it easier for them. I know we benefited from Mayo's involvement over the previous two years and I think Connacht will benefit from the fact that Galway won this year. Connacht teams don't have to be looking now in awe at other players like the Maurice Fitzgeralds or the Peter Canavans. People in the West can say 'o.k. we have a few guys down our neck of the woods that can provide role models for young players in Connacht'."

An answer perfectly put by a man whom many consider as their ideal role-model.

8

Player Speak

Kevin Cahill, Ballaghaderreen, Mayo

Losing a pair of All-Ireland finals is heartbreaking enough. Being out with long-term knee injury and missing one is even worse. Then, having worked your socks off to get back to full fitness, one game lost and the 1998 season is over. So reads Kevin Cahill's yo-yo inter-county career ever since he made a championship debut against Sligo in 1992. Abroad for the Galway-Kildare final, the 26-year-old Ballaghaderreen-based accountant rang home to get the result.

"I was in Italy on holiday and I rang home for the result. I was pleasantly surprised, though I was expecting Galway to do it. Kildare were over-rated. Galway had that sort of nice build-up. On the day they were deserving winners, no-one can dispute that. John O'Mahony had a big influence. From what I know of him he is a very disciplined sort of manager, very committed to organisational skills and stuff like that. He is very shrewd, he wouldn't give much away. Possibly his strongest point would be his organisational skills due to the fact there was a lot of key men who performed, who were able to carry the game to Kildare. Michael Donnellan, Ja Fallon...when you have one forward playing well it inspires all around. It has a domino effect on the team.

"You're delighted for Galway, yet you're sort of saying 'Christ, we were there twice and came back with nothing. They go up there one year and come home with the big prize'. If we got past Galway in the first round this year it might have been us. But I think the lads needed a break, too. They were a long time at it. They went over two seasons without a break so it had to get to them.

"Last year, I trained since Christmas just trying to get back for the game against Galway. I played a couple of challenge matches waiting for the championship. But you train so hard for five months, then all of a sudden one game and it was all over and all your hard work had gone out the window. It was very frustrating.

"I think an All-Ireland win was needed. We had come close a couple of years ago but still had not made the breakthrough. The national media has to give Connacht the credit they deserve having now actually made the breakthrough. You get to the All-Ireland and then you see the odds to win the All-Ireland the next year and you're down, you're in the middle of the group again. Obviously what you have to do to prove yourself is to win the All-Ireland. Coming second means nothing.

"It would be unbelievable to win an All-Ireland. It must be so emotional. Even coming back losing is so emotional. I'd say coming home winning would be just unbelievable, you wouldn't be able to describe it. 1996 was the one that got away. That one you still think about. You're driving to training and thinking 'Jaysus, if we had done it we wouldn't have to be going over here tonight'. Personally, myself, I remember Meath got a quick free the time Tommy Dowd scored the goal and I was on the goal-line and it went right between my legs. I'll never forget that as long as I live.

"Some players deal with the media interest better than others. I mean, coming up to the All-Ireland it can be a bit over-bearing. You're constantly on the phone at work, and at home even you just can't get away from it. You don't answer the phones. You say 'take a message, I'm not here. Take a message and I'll get back to you' and, of course, you never get back unless you want to. But if it wasn't there you'd sort of be giving out, too. We want both sides of the coin.

"As a young fella I didn't have much interest. My earliest memory is probably '89, going up to Dublin for the All-Ireland. Then I remember being in The Square in Ballaghaderreen for the celebration of getting to the All-Ireland that time. Gaelic football is a very enjoyable game. Round here it's the only game. You have to give it to the schools and the club for that. Everyone round here plays, there is no other sport to play. Ballaghaderreen is a great sort of town. You can support nearly anyone - Sligo, Roscommon, Galway or Mayo. This year, there was great interest in the championship all summer.

"It's going to be great. I think any team in Connacht can win the championship next year. The standard has come up, probably all over the country. Any team can win the All-Ireland but I think Connacht is extremely strong. You can see when Donegal won Ulster, you can see why Ulster teams kept it, kept the All-Ireland, and I think Galway winning the All-Ireland will inspire every other Connacht team and show what it means to them. They will raise their game. They have to beat Galway.

"Once they beat Galway they will have beaten the All-Ireland champions, so they will say 'why can't we be All-Ireland champions as well?'. That can only help Connacht football. Now teams are going up to win games rather than just give a good account of themselves. When you see the draw and see Galway you know this is the one. If you win you should get out of Connacht. It's the one you have to sort of peak for. But it's not really fair to say you get out of Connacht if you beat them. There's absolutely no easy game at all in the Connacht championship. There's no team you can take for granted. Even going over to London. Any team that takes London for granted could walk away from there with nothing.

"From a personal point of view I can't wait to get back into action. Manager John Maughan works us hard alright. He has brought in a lot of new players. This new talent is killing us in training. They're all fit and eager and hopefully they'll bring us all along. Young fellas give competition for places, they can raise everybody's game so the established lads know they've a fight on their hands to keep their places. It brings everything up a couple of steps if you get quality youngsters in."

*   *   *   *

Paul Coggins, Tír Chonaill Gaels, London

Perennial poor relations is how London have been viewed since their entry to the Connacht championship back in the seventies. Exiled in the English capital for the past nine years, Roscommon native Paul Coggins made his championship debut in 1997's close shave with Leitrim. Now the 32-year-old, self-employed with his own catering supply business based at Staples Corner, is eagerly awaiting next year's first round game with Galway at Ruislip. He watched this year's All-Ireland final in the Claddagh Ring pub in Hendon.

"The Claddagh Ring is one of the big Galway pubs. There was a good mixture but the people were mainly Galway. It was packed and there was a great atmosphere. I actually went out at half time. I had to make a phone call and I missed the first five to ten minutes, so I couldn't really believe the score when I came back. Galway were well-deserving of their victory. They were brilliant. I thought Michael Donnellan stood out. And the way they weren't afraid, they were like a team who weren't afraid to go for their destiny. Kildare looked as if they might pull away but Galway showed they had great spirit. It's a nice feeling to see a team from the West has finally done it. It will make the scene better. For Connacht it was what was badly needed. It's a great lift.

"Kildare were hot favourites over here, especially as people didn't have confidence in a team from the West, even though I thought they could do it myself. But we had Mayo, Sligo, Roscommon and Leitrim people all shouting for Galway that day. That's the one thing about it. You might even get some of the Leinster boys shouting for Connacht. You'll always find when a Connacht team is in it they'll shout for them. There were very big celebrations over here after the All-Ireland and it was people from all sides, people from all counties.

"Playing Galway next year is something to look forward to. To be honest, I mightn't have trained for another year only for the Galway thing. I would like to play against Galway if things work out. It'll be awful hard to give them a good game but playing the All-Ireland champions, it's a great thing to look forward to. There will be a huge crowd here that day, you'll have to come early, I'd say, to get in. The London Board are talking about it already and they have been making plans for it. I met a few of the Galway lads after the Connacht final replay and I was talking to Ray Silke and Ó Domhnaill and they were on about London football. They thought it was great we were still going. I'm sure it will be a great pleasure to play them.

"It's great to be in the Connacht championship, especially for a fella from the West of Ireland. It's special to be able to play no matter what happens. I hope it continues. The big help was that we got in the national league. I mean, it was really difficult to do well in the championship but the last couple of years we have shown improvement with the way we performed against Sligo and Leitrim. Even though we haven't done well in the league, it has helped us gain experience and when it came to championship we would put up a better performance than we maybe would have a few years back. That has helped and I hope we can be in the national league for a while.

"Sometimes in a paper we wouldn't even get a mention that we're in the Connacht championship. Mayo would be playing Roscommon in the semi-final even though Roscommon, say, would be playing London before that and they wouldn't mention it. But to be honest, we can't blame people for that because London took so many hammerings for maybe ten years that people don't take it serious. The breakthrough has to come, it's the only way. There's no point talking, action is the way to do it. It was a pity two years ago against Leitrim but I'd say people are taking more notice of us now.

"Leitrim was very frustrating. There was a piece done on it on *R.T.É.'s Sideline View* the following week and Eugene McGee said it wasn't right at all to play extra-time that day. It was very disappointing, a couple of decisions went against us. We played well that day. We should have at least got a draw, but you have to be very, very good to beat a Connacht team.

"You hear praise in dressingrooms after games and you appreciate it. Mickey Moran came in after the Sligo match and made a great speech and it wasn't patronising. He just said we performed well. It is great as long as people realise the effort is being put in over here. The commitment here is harder. Sometimes the traffic is terrible. You could be in South London doing a job or whatever and you'd have to get over to North London for training. And lads working in the city coming out on trains, going to training and then getting back home and it might be twelve o'clock. I know they do that over there, too, but I think travelling is a bigger commitment here because lads work later hours on average than they do in Ireland.

"People, first and foremost, come over here to make a living and there's a huge commitment to make to play football around that. I play for Tír Chonaill Gaels and for three years the commitment we put in was huge. There were lads from maybe fifty miles away travelling in and home at night. I know they do it in Ireland but what I'm saying is I think it's harder to do it here. We did well the last three years in the club championship. We never let ourselves down. We only lost to Knockmore by two points two years ago. It's the same with the London panel, too, there's great commitment.

"We'd like to get into a Connacht final someday. It mightn't happen straightaway, but with the younger lads from London coming through it might not be as far-fetched as people think. They have started a coaching course for young lads in London and they're going into schools, which is a great move. It's very important that we do get it together at under-age level because the flow of immigration is now to Ireland. There's a lot of teams broken up here. Like, hurling in Hertfordshire is totally gone now.

"I'm a big supporter of Roscommon. I went to the Connacht final replay this year and roared my head off for them. I have memories of Roscommon-Mayo matches. My father was from Mayo and I have memories of going with my young brothers with him to matches. He brought us to the All-Ireland final in 1980. We were up on Hill 16 and I remember being very scared because there was a huge crush when Roscommon got the goal. And I was thinking 'we're in trouble here if Roscommon win'. It was a mighty atmosphere that day. I remember it was a bit wet and I remember we were going home from Dublin that night and we were very depressed, very, very depressed even though we were only young at the time. I know Roscommon's Micheál Finneran over here in London. He was a great player and we have a talk about the 1980 final. I've great memories of that game."

*   *   *   *

George Dugdale, Mohill, Leitrim

Sunday, July 24th, 1994 heralded a shake up of Connacht's old order. Leitrim, for the first time in sixty seven years, had won the provincial title. Now a P.E. teacher based in Cavan Town, 30-year-old George Dugdale was one of the key ingredients in the triumph masterminded by John O'Mahony. It was a success not anticipated by the forward when he made his championship debut against London in 1987. This year's All-Ireland was seen at home on television.

"As a Connacht person, I was obviously hoping Galway would win and I was delighted that Galway did win. The better team won on the day. There can be no qualms about the fact they were the better team, especially in the second half. Maybe in the first half, the fifteen minutes before half-time, they had a bad patch, but apart from that they were on top and deservedly won. It was a good game, especially in the second half when Galway hit that purple-patch, played some fabulous football and took some brilliant long range scores. It was superb. The fact they were underdogs going into the game helped them a good lot because there was a lot of pressure off them. Kildare were made such strong favourites and the occasion, to a certain extent, got to them as well. There was a lot of pressure on them. But having said that, Galway played the more direct football and they took their chances when they came. Their direct style of play was a factor in winning. There was also a lot of pressure on the Kildare players in trying to work the ball short, the way they normally play. Galway forced Kildare to make the mistakes.

"I don't think mixed emotions came into it this year because we were comprehensively beaten by Galway in Carrick. Possibly there was mixed emotions in the Leitrim players when we lost to Galway back in 1995 as that was the year we slipped up and possibly missed out on an All-Ireland final appearance. That would be the only sense of mixed emotions from a Leitrim perspective. Galway were clinical in everything they did against us in June but their performance was helped by the fact that Leitrim played so poorly and didn't really perform. It was mystifying as to what happened to us. We just totally collapsed and they punished us for every mistake we made. The fact we played badly was compounded by Galway really playing well that day. It was hard to draw anything from that game because we played so poorly. It was a major down because there was such a good atmosphere among the players. Training had been going well, results in challenge matches were satisfying and we went into the game confident we could maybe make an upset. We knew to do so we had to play to our potential but we didn't even perform that day. The team was going through transition this year with new players coming in and maybe the occasion got to them. And maybe the fact that some of the senior players, myself included, didn't play near to our potential - we just weren't good enough on the day.

"John O'Mahony had them prepared mentally for the occasion and they are talented players. They have good balance between young and senior players, so Carrick didn't hold any fears for them, especially on the back of beating Mayo who had reached the All-Ireland for the two years previously. John was one of the main reasons Galway did win the All-Ireland. Results speak for themselves. Galway hadn't been in an All-Ireland final since '83. They always had an abundance of talent there, it was just getting the right person in there to get the right talent together working cohesively as a unit and he did that. He got everybody together and I suppose proper training, preparation...the way he prepares teams he's meticulous in everything he does, organisation, preparation, be it mental or physical, building up team spirit...all those things he's very good at and he used the same approach in Galway this year. He had a good bunch of players which helps.

"It was absolutely brilliant in 1994. John was probably the best manager I've ever played under. Just the way he went about his job, he was totally professional and no stone was left unturned so the team was prepared as best as possible for whatever game we were playing. The preparation we did was intense. We prepared mentally as well for games and he built a good bond among the players. He had a good friendship with us and brought self-belief that we could maybe win a Connacht championship. He commanded a lot of self-respect. All these things put together add up to being a good manager.

"There was the perception that Leitrim, when it came to championship, were a hard luck story. We'd push teams for sixty minutes, then lose in the last ten. Some players were happy with that. Supporters were happy we pushed 'x', 'y' and 'z' to within two points and they went and got to the All-Ireland or whatever. John brought in a whole new perspective. We had it in our hands to change if we followed the guidelines he was setting down. What he was putting down for us was to pursue a Connacht title and that we could do it. He built confidence, created mental toughness and so forth - we did believe we could win a Connacht title.

"I have a lot of good memories of '94 that it's hard to pick one. Every game was a battle, a major step for us bearing in mind our lack of success in championship. I suppose the Connacht final day in Hyde Park, the sense of emotion we'd won it would stand out. Then going to play in Croke Park, it was a dream of the players to go and play in an All-Ireland semi-final. Other memories are the homecoming, the Monday after the Connacht final and going all over the different towns. Coming to Mohill, it was actually very emotional.

"All youngsters follow successful teams, and as a youngster growing up I was a fan of that Dublin team of the seventies and early eighties. The fact that Leitrim football was going nowhere, I didn't have a team to follow as such. Results are what speak and with Connacht teams going to Croke Park and getting hammered it was easy to say that Connacht teams were afraid to go there. Ulster teams going to Croke Park were whipping boys for a while but then they turned it around in the nineties and won four All-Irelands. Maybe it's Connacht football's turn now. With Galway winning the All-Ireland and a Galway team winning the club championship, there's no derogatory statements about the standard of Connacht football at the minute. Possibly Mayo could have won an All-Ireland as well. Connacht football is up there with the best at the minute.

"Obviously Galway are the favourites next year. When you're champions you're up there and everybody wants to beat you. You give that extra bit to try and knock champions and I suppose the fact that Galway won the All-Ireland this year gives teams a great incentive to go and replicate that in years ahead.

"Leitrim winning the Connacht minor title and the U-21s doing so well this year was a boost. Minors are your team of the future and it was great to see them getting to the All-Ireland semi-final, despite the fact they were sort of overwhelmed on the day. It was a great shot in the arm for Leitrim football that they did get to the semi-final. On the back of such a bad senior performance it was something for the supporters to cheer about. The fact that there seems to be talent coming through is promising and encouraging."

*   *   *   *

Eamonn O'Hara, Tourlestrane, Sligo

Galway proved this year that Gaelic football has fast become a young man's game. But youth having its day had been a policy in vogue in Sligo for the past number of years. At the age of eighteen, Eamonn O'Hara was given a 1994 championship debut against Mayo. Four years on, the 23-year-old has become a pivotal figure in Sligo's recent resurgence. In both 1995 and 1996, they took Galway to unfruitful replays following drawn games they should have won. The same happened with Roscommon in 1998. And in 1997, Sligo reached a Connacht final for the first time since 1975 only to lose to Mayo by a point. Seated in the front row of the Cusack Stand, Eamonn, a bank official, was one of Galway's most vociferous supporters at this year's All-Ireland final.

"September 27th was a great day, a great day for Connacht football, a long time coming. Mayo had been there for the last two years and to see Galway going on and doing it, it was just excellent. Realistically, Mayo could have won it the last two years, so it means you can say the last three years Connacht football has come on an awful lot. It was just a great achievement for Galway, for Connacht football. There was huge excitement. I attend the All-Irelands every other year but the fact there was a Connacht team there and not ranked favourites on the day and to go out and play the type of football that they played was a joy to see.

"Tomás Mannion was my man of the match. During the championship he looked good and definitely, on the day, Martin Lynch wasn't up to scratch for him. I felt that Ja Fallon had to play from the start rather than the last twenty minutes like he had played throughout the championship. Glen Ryan did do a good job on him in the first half, but Jarlath played brilliantly in the second half. Michael Donnellan had an absolute cracker. He constantly worked around the field. His workrate was unbelievable. And the way he took some of his scores was a joy to see, too. But it was an overall victory for the team. Midfield did well and the goalkeeper had a very cute game.

"John O'Mahony proved with all teams he has managed, like Mayo and Leitrim, he won two Connacht titles with them and now he's done it with Galway, that he has a special touch. It is his preparation, the way he coaches players. He works on individual players as well as the team. If a man needs to improve his shooting that's what he'll work on. He's got something special to rise lads, to get them going at the right time. The final word is down to the players. If they don't do it on the field it's a waste of time. It's a big effort from all sides, but O'Mahony does have something special.

"The media said it was great Sam Maguire has come across to Connacht for one year. It had broken the duck. Now they say it's going to be a Leinster team, a Munster team or Ulster team next year. Basically, the long-term attitude is that Sam's stay in Connacht is very, very short. I think the praise for Connacht football is very slack. The media are still going on saying Mayo were a poor team and whatever else. But they got to the final two years in succession. Few teams have done that in recent years.

"When Donegal won in '92 they brought it down to Sligo. It was an eye-opener that time to get it that close to home, to see all the celebrations and that. Donegal won it out of the blue. No-one was expecting them to win it. They trained exceptionally hard and won an All-Ireland. Sligo did celebrate the win with Donegal. They were a team, like ourselves, that had never won it. It was something special for them. We looked at ourselves and said 'geez, we could do that. No problem'. It's just a case of going out and doing the work. There's no reason why we can't do it. We took a lot of heart from that. Anyone can win an All-Ireland now, it's a case of proving it.

"Mickey Moran came in as manager and he introduced the different brand of football which was a support passing, hand passing game so far and then the long ball up to let the ball do the work after that. He brought in a new system of playing football and he brought a different type of belief. He really believed in us, travelling from Derry. He wasn't coming down to waste time. We took from the fact that he was travelling so far for training, that he did believe in us and we started to believe in ourselves.

"In the 1997 Connacht final, Mayo, on the day, were outright favourites and we felt that we had absolutely nothing to lose. It was like the All-Ireland this year, Kildare were ranked favourites. We'd got to a Connacht final, which was a great achievement for us, and we felt we could win it. Mayo was our bogey team for many years and we wanted to break the duck. They had beaten us heavily in many championship games. We had a young team, we'd no fear and we were getting sick of the attitude of losing. Our attitude going in there was totally focussed on winning, nothing else. It wasn't the best game of football. We felt that if the referee had played the full injury-time you don't know what would have happened. Maybe we mightn't have deserved to win the game but we might have deserved to get a second bite at the cherry.

"We were strong enough in Hyde Park against Roscommon this year. They came back from seven points down and we were lucky to get a draw with them that day, in the end. But we felt there and then we should have won. We deserved to win. It was only in the last ten minutes Roscommon started to play football. But in the replay they had their homework done. We sort of lined out a different team than usual and it didn't happen for us on the day. Then Roscommon should have beaten Galway over the two days. They were the best team between the two of them. Roscommon were very unlucky that way, but if you want to go back and back you'd say we were very unlucky not to be in that final. It's a tight line between success and loss which is great, great for Connacht football.

"It's a young man's game now. Pat Spillane said recently there was only two on the Galway team married and only two people on the Kerry team that won it last year married. It's gone that way. It's a young man's game. The height of fitness now is unbelievable, it's gone so professional. It has changed an awful lot and a lot of young lads are coming in and working hard. With the younger lads I don't think they have any fear until after a number of years. They don't know what to expect. They just go out and play their best football on the day. Older lads that are probably struggling with injuries and fitness, they're finding it hard to compete with the younger lads. We've had Bernie Mulhern retire. He's only thirty or thirty one. Twenty years ago if you were thirty or thirty one, you could have played until at least thirty six if you were able to play.

"We don't care who we play next year, it makes no difference to us. We just going to have to prove we're good enough. We feel we can beat anybody in Connacht. I know it's a cocky attitude to have, but Mayo have been living that high attitude saying they could beat anybody, which they can when when they want to. We're trying to develop that kind of attitude so we can beat anyone in Connacht. It's an attitude you have to try and work on and believe in yourself."

*   *   *   *

Tom Ryan, Boyle, Roscommon

Talk about encountering the 1998 All-Ireland finalists from both sides of the fence. A colossus in his own side's nerve-wracking Connacht final encounters with Galway, Tom Ryan, by dint of being an army captain based at The Curragh and living in Naas, was left to also watch Kildare prepare for their big day. The 27-year-old, who made his championship debut against Leitrim in 1993, watched the final in Boyle having opted to give his father his match ticket.

"Kildare had gone absolutely mad up here. The whole place was togged out in white. The talk everywhere was of tickets, they were nearly impossible to get. Fellas were in draws, approaching clubs and they were looking for anyone outside that might have a ticket to bring to them. Really, they were desperate for tickets and I'd say that people that didn't even normally go to matches were all caught up in it. I was talking to John Finn afterwards and he said going into training and coming out of training the first week of the build-up they were unsettled because you couldn't get in or out without fifteen minutes giving autographs and that sort of *craic*. It was gone absolutely mental but it calmed down for them afterwards. But it was such a build up because people were talking about how long Glen Ryan would go on in his after-match speech...crazy stuff altogether. They were really expecting a win.

"I actually thought Kildare had the game won until the second half. Before the game I thought Galway could do it. People up in Kildare were saying 'well, what are the Galway team like?'. They were kind of wondering how they were around midfield. And before the game I would have said the strongest area for Kildare was midfield and I thought it was there they could do it, but I thought Galway had the more dangerous forwards. You can say its sixty years or whatever since Kildare won it but I thought Galway would be more hungry and they would have more bite. And I was thinking that if we were there that's the attitude we would have. Galway seemed to manage midfield perfectly. They got around the long kick-outs. The goalkeeper's kick-outs were perfect. They got round that problem and they really took over in the second half. But I genuinely thought at half-time they weren't going to win it. And then they just took over. Kildare were just rocked for fifteen or twenty minutes and they just lost it. Galway seemed to get better. They weren't relying on one or two fellas to score. Even Ó Domhnaill scored...it just seemed to all work for them on the day, fellas that wouldn't normally score, we'll say. They had a better gel in the team.

"John O'Mahony comes across as the type of guy who seems to be very well-organised. There was small little things mentioned during the game where the commentator said that Galway had gone and played a challenge game the week before and the opposition had worn white jersies. They'd gone up to Croke Park, checked out their dressing room. They're all small details but I'm sure it puts all the players' minds at ease doing those kind of things. You know to go up to see it beforehand and know where you're going, it would take away that sense of awe when you're looking round not having done it before. Johno seems to be very well-organised. He thinks out his game plan well. I mean, Kevin Walsh caught six or seven balls in front of McCreery with short kick-outs and they'd obviously planned for it. They were tactics that worked for them so he seems a shrewd manager. That's all small stuff but it all builds a bigger picture. It shows the sign of someone who thinks about all angles. He is very thorough in his preparation.

"It was a pity that all the excitement has to be in the West when a Western team wins. Galway won it and got great credit for it and now it seems to have died down. It doesn't matter what a Connacht team seems to do there's just that attitude there that Connacht football seems to be behind, despite the fact that Mayo were up there for two years in a row and Galway now have won it. It just doesn't seem to get the real sort of credit whereas when the North were strong and were winning, it was a case of the North being the strongest province and there was plenty about it. But there's not a huge amount about the Connacht scene as a result. It was even reflected in the International Rules thing, there were only a handful of Connacht lads in it. It was good to see a few of the Galway lads brought in late on. They were getting recognised for their achievement and it crowned the year for a couple of them anyway.

"I was watching the All-Ireland at home and it was kind of with mixed feelings. I know a lot of the Galway lads from U.C.G. - Finnegan, de Paor was the captain that year we won it, Gary Fahy and all those guys, and there was a certain amount of jealousy watching them going up to collect their medals. But when you sit back and look at it, it's good that a Connacht team has won it now. But while I was supporting them, it was a killer knowing we could have been there because we were so close to them. All you're thinking all the time was 'what would we be at now, where would we be going or how would we be preparing for it'. You often complain about the travelling but when we got on a roll, everybody was looking forward to it. Not one player was cribbing. Then watching the other teams progressing, you read all the reports. It gets to you. You're wondering 'geez, it's a pity we weren't there'. I'm not saying we'd have got that far, but we'd have liked to have thought that had we got out of Connacht we'd have got by Derry and into an All-Ireland final. That's in the back of your mind all the time. But when you've time to get a reflection on it, it was good to see Galway brought it back.

"In extra-time at Roscommon, Fallon seemed to come into his own. He got three points in the first period of extra-time. He had been quiet the whole game but he's that sort of player. Again when I was discussing it with the Kildare lads up here, he was one of the guys they were always asking me about. Now Glen Ryan had a very good first half but I reckoned no matter how strong he played, he was never going to keep Fallon quiet for the whole game. Fallon had a quiet enough first half but still came into his own in the second half, scoring a few brilliant points. He was one of the players who did damage against us in the replay.

"There's a huge amount to look forward to next year. We'll be going out with great expectations. Mayo are kind of gone quiet, they're gone a year now, but at the same time they'll be looking to come out as well. We narrowly beat Sligo. The only team that's weak at the moment is Leitrim. It was the poorest Leitrim team I've seen playing in a good while. Normally when you go to Carrick-on-Shannon you come out of there well-bruised if you win it. Other than that the other teams are all pretty much on a par. You have the added bonus if you're playing Galway now, you're playing the All-Ireland champions. With the bite that would be in it because we lost to them, if we got up against them it would be great. That's the way we're thinking. If you could actually beat the champions, it would raise your confidence.

"I remember very little of the 1980 All-Ireland. I can remember watching that one on the television. I remember not thinking too much of Pat Spillane after that, he wasn't doing us any favours dropping down to the ground whenever he could. But there was great excitement. The All-Ireland is a mighty day out. You would love to think that someday we'll get to actually be on the other side of it and play in one. It'd be fabulous."

9

The Board Room

Galway's watershed victory has rippled through Connacht G.A.A circles. County Boards across the province have, at last, a real benchmark in which to measure the progress of their senior teams. G.A.A. brethren in the West, for so long, had to peer into the backyard of other provinces in order to get a glimpse of what is necessary to compete at the highest level. Now, finally, that role-model is on their own door-steps.

John O'Mahony's training techniques may still remain confidential but other teams in Connacht at least have the opportunity of rubbing shoulders with the All-Ireland champions in next year's championship. That, in itself, will provide huge motivation for Mayo, Roscommon, Sligo, Leitrim, London and newcomers New York in their preparations for 1999. It is a summer that looks set to be the most thrilling for G.A.A. supporters in the province for a long, long time.

Whatever of the keen rivalry down through the years, it is also clear that Galway's neighbours are extremely proud of what has been achieved in 1998. After decades of disappointment, this All-Ireland victory has reconstructed the depressing image of Connacht football, restoring it to its former glory and stature among its more illustrious counterparts. Galway have not only injected pride back into their own county, they have struck an immeasurable blow for the resurgence of Connacht football. It is fitting therefore that their neighbours are at the forefront in paying tribute to their marvellous success.

In this chapter, G.A.A. officials from the five Connacht counties reveal their fond thoughts and positive insights on Galway's glory and what it will mean for the welfare of Connacht football in the future.

*   *   *   *

Outgoing chairman of the Roscommon County Board, Tommie Kenoy has held the office for the last nine years. P.R.O. from 1983 to 1986 before becoming vice-chairman of the Board, he was elected to his current position in 1990. A member of the Kilmore club, Tommie trained the senior team to their first county final in eleven years last October, only to be defeated by Roscommon Gaels.

"Galway's victory is a huge shot in the arm for Connacht football and I believe that a couple of All-Irelands will come to the West in the years ahead as a result. All the Connacht counties will now believe they can emulate that feat. The management structure which Galway put in place was the key difference. Even the most talented group of players will underachieve without organisation and back-up of the required standard, and Galway seemed to have a very professional set-up this year. John O'Mahony's organisational skills, his professionalism and his attention to detail appear to be his most important managerial qualities.

"The two-and-a-half games against Roscommon were the making of the Galway team. There is no substitute for the experiences to be gained in hard championship football and Roscommon asked some tough questions which taught Galway a great deal about themselves. As regards how good a side Galway are, it will only be answered in the next couple of years.

"There is another All-Ireland in this team, although its going to be difficult for them. If we look back at the 1973 Cork team for example: everybody was predicting they would win several All-Irelands but it never happened. So much will depend on how Galway adjust to the burden of being champions and of course, how much hunger and ambition they have. O'Mahony's professionalism will make a difference in this context, however, and I think they will win another. It's certainly going to be a fascinating championship next year and Galway can expect a major challenge to their title within their own province.

"Galway's three-in-a-row was among my earliest sporting memories but it's not really possible to make a valid comparison with them, as the game has moved a long way since then. The current team has a long way to go before it can claim the same status in the nineties as the sixties team had in their era."

Roscommon County Board secretary for the last five years, Tom Mullaney was previously vice-chairman for four years. The Shannon Gaels clubman was also chairman of the Board for six years in the seventies, and in the eighties he was a member of the county history committee which assisted in the completion of a detailed history of Roscommon, published in 1990.

"This year was an outstanding one for Connacht football. Galway's win in the All-Ireland confirmed what many had believed within the province: that our standard was much higher than we got credit for. The lead-up to Galway's win was Mayo playing in All-Irelands in the last two years and definitely they should have won at least one of them.

"Roscommon didn't look a likely threat for fifty five minutes against Sligo in their opening tie but they emerged as lucky enough, one-point winners after the following fifteen minutes and the subsequent one hour and ten minutes in Sligo. It did not give any indication though that they would threaten Galway in the final.

"The Connacht final was probably the best training experience Galway had all year. Those two matches stood them when they won the All-Ireland semi-final and eventually the final. The Connacht final, over two matches, tested their character time and time again and it showed in the subsequent games. The All-Ireland champions being from Connacht cannot but augur well for the Connacht championship in 1999 and it should be one of the best championships for years.

"John O'Mahony's role in Galway's success cannot be underestimated, though 'Bosco' McDermott and Val Daly brought Galway and a talented bunch of players to a certain level. In having John as manager, however, the team acquired experience through him winning provincial titles with Mayo and Leitrim and this experience proved invaluable for Galway in winning the ultimate honours.

"There are comparisons with this present team and the three-in-a-row team but whether they prove to be as good, time will tell. Interestingly, in 1963, before Galway's three-in-a-row, that team, with approximately the same number of U-21 players, should have won an All-Ireland but lost to Dublin."

*   *   *   *

Current chairman of the Mayo County Board, P.J. McGrath was previously Connacht Council chairman for three years and formerly chairman of the provincial coaching committee. The Kilmaine clubman is a former referee and was the man in the middle for the famous 1982 All-Ireland football final between Offaly and Kerry. He is also a current trustee of the G.A.A. in Croke Park.

"Winning an All-Ireland is a wonderful achievement for a comparatively young county team and they will be around for many years yet. Their All-Ireland final display was a highlight. They played Gaelic football as it should be played and once they overcame Mayo in the first round, I knew they would be hard-stopped. This win is firm evidence that Connacht football is as good as any. This is evidenced by Mayo's participation in the last two All-Irelands and Galway's victory this year. It's also justification for the policy of coaching adopted by the Connacht Council during the nineties.

"The difference for Galway in 1998 was that they adopted a new approach, spurred on by Corofin's famous victory in the All-Ireland club final earlier in the year.

"They introduced a new manager, new players and a new belief in themselves. John O'Mahony is one of the leading managers in Gaelic football, very meticulous in his attention to detail and he succeeds in having his team very well-focussed at all times.

"Comparing the current team with the sixties teams is a case of different teams with different styles. My memories of Galway winning three-in-a-row are Noel Tierney's famous high catches which sadly are not now part of the modern passing game.

"There is another All-Ireland in this present team and they must be favourites to retain all their crowns next year. It's one tag that John O'Mahony won't like but one he will overcome.

"With Galway as defending champions, it will add great bite to future encounters. There was never much need to add anything to games between Mayo and Galway because they were all classics but we look forward to kicking the ball out to them next year."

Sean Feeney, from the Ballintubber G.A.A. club, was elected secretary of the Mayo County Board in December 1994. Serving ten years as assistant secretary before that, he was also formerly secretary of the West Mayo G.A.A. Board for eleven years. During his playing career, he played in goals for Mayo junior footballers and he is a brother of former senior player, Ger Feeney.

"Galway's win has given Connacht football self-belief and now that they have made the breakthrough, at least three Connacht teams will win All-Irelands in the next five years.

"The difference this year for Galway was the ingredients for success: good players; accurate forwards; good management; the ability to win some games without having to extend oneself; getting through a season 'injury-free' and luck. John O'Mahony's is also very focussed, meticulous, organised and experienced. This current Galway team is young and skilful and there is another All-Ireland in this team. But next year's Connacht championship will be very competitive - any one of the five counties can win it.

"As regards memories of Galway winning the famous three-in-a-row, I remember John Donnellan coming in with the Sam Maguire to St. Jarlaths, Tuam. Comparing that side and the current team, the game is much faster now and I think it's as good if not better than those times."

*   *   *   *

Sligo County Board chairman for the last three years, Joe Queenan is a current selector on Mickey Moran's management team. Before becoming County chairman, he held the position of vice-chairman for seven years. Also chairman of the West Divisional Board from 1985-1989, Joe served as chairman of his own Enniscrone/Kilglass club from 1985 to 1995.

"Galway are a very good team and were great ambassadors for Connacht football in 1998. I was in the Hogan Stand for the final and the people from the other four counties were very proud when Ray Silke lifted the Sam Maguire. Their win is a tremendous boost for Connacht football and it proves that the standard of football here is as good if not better than in any other province at the moment. It will also give a great lift to all the people who are promoting the game in the province.

"The difference this year for Galway has been a number of things - John O'Mahony, two big men in the middle of the field, Ja Fallon and Niall Finnegan back in the panel and the five U-21 players that made it on to the senior team. John O'Mahony is a brilliant manager and a real nice guy. He had his players exceptionally fit, focussed and well-organised on the field.

"I have no memories of Galway winning the famous three-in-a-row because it was before my time. But I saw a video of the 1966 final and I thought there was far more catch and kick than the present day. Today's game is much faster and there is far more pressure on players, managers and County Boards. The Connacht championship will be one of the most exciting championship in years, with any county good enough to win it."

Sligo County Board's Tommy Kilcoyne, from the St. Nathys club in Mullinabreena, is the longest-serving secretary in the province, holding the office for the last twenty eight years. His late father, Tommie was also county secretary from 1924 to 1968 and Connacht Council secretary from 1934 to 1968. The Connacht minor football trophy is named after his father.

"Galway's All-Ireland win in 1998 was a marvellous achievement. I have very good memories of their win over Mayo in McHale Park in May as Sligo won the Connacht junior football championship title for the first time in twenty five years in the curtain-raiser to that game.

"The two Connacht finals were memorable. The rain and wind of Tuam Stadium was a real test for both teams that day and they served up a fine contest. The Saturday evening epic replay at Hyde Park was a wonderful advertisement for Connacht football and I really believe it set up Galway for their All-Ireland attempt. The semi-final win over Derry said more about the traditional Galway in Croke Park than anything else. Galway also seem to go to Croke Park expecting to win, at least it was always like that in the sixties.

"But talk about keeping the best wine 'til last. Galway's display on All-Ireland day was exceptional, the best I have seen since Donegal scored eighteen points in the 1992 final when Brian McEniff's men brought the Sam Maguire on a memorable journey to the North West. The youthful exuberance of Michael Donnellan, the skills of Jarlath Fallon, Padraic Joyce's clinically finished goal and Seán Óg de Paor's two invaluable points are the memories that will stay with me.

"My initial reaction to Galway's win was one of delight that the Sam Maguire was returning to Connacht after a lapse of thirty two years. I am particularly pleased for everybody involved in football in Galway. It also gives much hope to all the other counties in Connacht. In Sligo, we believe that if we had qualified for this year's Connacht final, we would have run Galway just as close as Roscommon did. Remember also that many of the present Galway team, including Gary Fahy, Seán Óg de Paor, Tomás Mannion, Ray Silke, Jarlath Fallon, Fergal Gavin, Niall Finnegan and others, came to Markievicz Park in 1995 and 1996. We drew with them on each occasion before losing replays in Tuam Stadium.

"It's impossible to say with certainty what made the difference this year with Galway. Everything seemed to fall into place. Exceptional planning, excellent players, the replayed Connacht final, the skills of John O'Mahony, the groundwork done by 'Bosco' McDermott, Val Daly and others, and the emergence of young players like Michael Donnellan. All these played a part. Also, the wonderful support by Galway fans. Whatever it was. The mix was just right. I have the utmost respect for John O'Mahony and heartily congratulate him on his wonderful achievements in 1998. His record with Mayo, Leitrim and now Galway is exceptional and will probably never be equalled. To win Connacht championships with three different counties is remarkable.

"He seems to have the happy knack of getting teams to play to their strengths. His tactical awareness in the All-Ireland final was spot on and played a huge part in the win. It's always difficult to make the right decisions in the white heat of a championship match but to get everything just right in an All-Ireland final, as John did, is a real vindication of his abilities as a manager.

"As a student in U.C.G. in the mid-sixties, I have many memories of Galway's three-in-a-row. Enda Colleran, Pat and John Donnellan, Christy Tyrell, Martin Newell, Mattie McDonagh and the rest. What wonderful footballers they were and they seemed so unassuming about it all. The Connacht final of 1965 comes to mind, right in the middle of the three-in-a-row period. Sligo led them well in Tuam Stadium but were caught before the finish. Another one that got away. Did Cyril Dunne ever miss a free? Did Johnny Geraghty ever let in a goal? Those were fabulous years for Galway football and who could have forecast then that it would take them thirty two years to win again.

"Is there another All-Ireland in this team? That's a very difficult question. The recent pattern in the nineties is that it takes such a supreme effort to win one that it's impossible to repeat it the following year. My hope is that Sligo will make a breakthrough in Connacht in 1999. We are the only Connacht county without a provincial senior football championship in the nineties and we have only one chance left to remedy that. With Galway as defending champions, the Connacht Council should book Croke Park for next year's Connacht championship. Every match in it will be a crowd puller and a cracker.

*   *   *   *

Chairman of the Leitrim County Board for the last three years, Des Quinn worked alongside John O'Mahony's management team in the 1995-1996 season. The Aughawillan clubman previously held the position of vice-chairman, also for three years.

"I was delighted to see Galway as a Connacht team capture the All-Ireland after such a long wait. I think the All-Ireland final itself was the highlight. In particular, the style of play adopted by Galway was in many ways a breath of fresh air - a minimum amount of short passing with the emphasis on foot passing and quick direct ball. Personally, I thought Tomás Mannion was man of the match with an absolutely exemplary display at corner-back. Ja Fallon's high catch in the second half and Michael Donnellan's solo run and point were particularly memorable.

"Obviously, Galway got everything right. In particular, they got the right blend of players - skilful, fast forwards, a tight-marking defence and an imposing midfield pairing. They also got a good management team that knew their players and knew how to get the best out of them. Galway also received a lot of confidence from a very successful run in the national league before being defeated by Offaly at the quarter-final stage. It allowed sufficient time to readjust and re-focus.

"Lastly, there was an air of confidence in the Galway camp, particularly after their win over Mayo and the success of Corofin that made them feel they had the ability to go that one step further. This win is just the kind of fillip that Connacht football badly needed. With Mayo losing the previous two finals, there was a feeling that Connacht teams had not got the bottle to go all the way. Now that bogey is out of the way it will mean that other Connacht teams that reach the latter stages will have a new belief and confidence in themselves.

"To manage a team to All-Ireland success is the ultimate accolade any team manager in the country would want to achieve. John is a deserving recipient. Having learned his trade with his native Mayo and later with Leitrim, he was well-equipped to take on the Galway job. From the start, John knew the talent was there in abundance. His organisational ability and his ability to pick a good management team allowed him to carry out his plans in great detail. It is the attention to detail that sets him apart. He always gains tremendous respect from his players and he puts huge emphasis on the role of the team captain.

"Looking back at the three-in-a-row team, it is difficult to compare teams from different eras. Today's game is obviously much faster but Galway's three-in-a-row team was special. They came on the scene when television was replaced by radio in homes around the country and All-Irelands were being seen live for the first time. For young players of our era, all the Galway players were heroes.

"There is no doubt that the present team compares well with that team. Whether they can go on to win further All-Irelands or a three-in-a-row is impossible to predict. Nowadays, because the standard has levelled off, it much more difficult to win successive All-Irelands, simply because the commitment required to achieve that is awesome. There is no doubt that this team is capable of winning another All-Ireland. When is the difficult question. Previous winners in recent years have all found it next to impossible to come back and win a second title.

"Next year's Connacht championship will be extremely competitive. Great interest will focus on next year's draw. Obviously, everybody will wish to avoid Galway but Mayo and Roscommon, after last season, will feel they are very close to the mark. Sligo are also in there and will not be underestimated. Leitrim have probably the biggest gap to close as they are in a team-building process. Nonetheless, they will be keen to do well like everybody else."

Tommy Moran, a member of the Leitrim back-room, headed by John O'Mahony, is another of the long-serving secretaries in Connacht, having served in the same office since 1982. Formerly a Central Council delegate from 1975-1982, Tommy was also a referee in his day.

"Galway's win was certainly a morale-booster for Connacht, although it is a little worrying for Connacht that they are the only team from the province to have won an All-Ireland in a period of fifty years.

"They could have easily lost to Mayo or Roscommon, as their hardest games on their journey to the All-Ireland were within Connacht. They had bits of luck against Mayo and Roscommon, but you need that to win.

"John O'Mahony's side looked super against Leitrim but looked very ordinary in the Connacht final and replay. They also looked in trouble in the second quarter in the All-Ireland but they turned on the style when the chips were down. Padraic Joyce's point just before half-time was important - had he missed it, I felt Kildare would have won.

"This win will make it a bumper 1999 Connacht championship. Galway play London in the first round and a full house in Ruislip is guaranteed. If it's Galway against Leitrim, then our side will have to redeem pride while Mayo will want revenge if they are pitted against their old rivals. Sligo will also not be overawed if they meet the All-Ireland champions, while Roscommon will have no hang-ups and will be tough opposition again.

"Looking at the difference this year, Galway's pride would have been dented, losing to Leitrim in 1993 and 1994. They only had about three hundred supporters in Carrick when they beat us in 1995 but they went on to win Connacht and do well in the All-Ireland semi-final versus Tyrone. So, the base of the team was there but they just needed a few more players and perhaps more organisation.

"Getting six players from the U-21 team was a major boost this year and wouldn't any county love that. John O'Mahony also brought confidence, organisation and professionalism into the side. When he makes a commitment to something, he simply never switches off. He is consumed in his mind about players, training facilities, medical treatment, fitness, travel arrangements, availability of players and the attitude of players as a unit. Of course, there is also a big emphasis on back-up facilities for the team. He is also very much into mind games and how to treat players in even the smallest detail so as to get the best out of them. John is constantly thinking, planning and using psychology.

"Maybe a computer could but you can't compare teams of thirty years ago with present day teams. Leitrim people of my age and older have many memories of Galway in the late fifties when Leitrim lost out to the great Purcell-Stockwell teams in four successive Connacht finals. The three-in-a-row team swept though Connacht and looked a team of All-Stars but at that stage, there were massive gaps between a few top teams and the rest. That gap has now been closed.

"Do I think there is another All-Ireland in this team? Will any team ever win two All-Irelands in a row again? The day of a few dominating teams is gone. This Galway team could win another All-Ireland but probably not next year. It is difficult to retain even a provincial title and there are so many other teams who would fancy themselves as champions. I have no doubt that John O'Mahony is already working on 1999, so who knows?

"The Connacht championship will be a cliffhanger next season but from a Leitrim point of view, we certainly will be looking for a different performance from our team. Come the championship draw, maybe we will all have a better idea!"

*   *   *   *

Experiencing the ecstasy of an All-Ireland victory must be a magnificent feeling but Galway County Board chairman, Pat Egan, has had the special pleasure of also seeing his own Corofin club capture All-Ireland club honours in the same year. What a truly enviable position to be in! County chairman for the last eight years, Pat previously spent eight years as vice-chairman, seven years as chairman of the North Board and three years as chairman of his own club.

"It was always a dream of mine to be part of a county team to win an All-Ireland but to be chairman of the Board and see Galway produce Connacht's first All-Ireland in thirty two years was unbelievable. I had great hopes after beating Mayo, and the Galway supporters sensed it too. That win over Mayo really set us on the way. Then the draw with Roscommon and the replay helped us in no small way to give our team the experience to go and win the All-Ireland. When we defeated Roscommon after two great games, I believed we were ready for Croke Park.

"This All-Ireland win opens a door for Connacht football as before we were not taken seriously, and at even at times, we were belittled. Now we have everyone asking how we did it. When we brought the cup across The Shannon, I was amazed to see all the other counties of Connacht represented on the bridge of Athlone. No longer will Galway, or any other county in Connacht, be wary of playing in Croke Park, or be afraid to win.

"Looking at the players, we certainly had a good squad and a fine mix of experience and youth. The Galway Football Board decided to put the best possible management structure in place. We went outside Galway for the first time and chose a winner in John O'Mahony as manager. John organised a fine team to complement him in terms of selectors, medical people etc...

"We knew John had done the business with Mayo and Leitrim and we liked his style of man-management and attention to detail. Little did we realise how meticulous the man was.

"He was essential to our All-Ireland win and no matter what the crises, he was ice-cool and in command during the tough test against Roscommon in the Connacht final. He was the same at half-time in the All-Ireland final. When things were not going that well in the first half, he stood out and proved the great man he is. Some would call him the ice-man but I see him as an honest gentleman.

"I remember the three-in-a-row team well, they were a colossal team and a fine bunch of men. But let's face it, this team of ours can hold their heads high alongside any team, even the three-in-a-row. This is a young team and we may or may not win more All-Irelands but we will certainly be in the shake-up again - and soon with the help of God.

"The Connacht championship in 1999 will be the most competitive for years. We know how close the counties of Connacht are to us, there were two draws in the '98 championship. Just a few points separated the teams. We know that a lot of those teams will be waiting in the long grass with a desire to knock Galway of their lofty perch. We will try to hold on to our laurels but if someone beats us, we will be the first to shake their hands.

"My overall thoughts of this achievement centre on my feelings of being All-Ireland champions and on how lovely and sincere the comments I, as chairman, received from all quarters inside and outside Galway. We feel so humble and yet so proud of the manner in which we won, and we are thankful to have played such a wonderful and sporting team as Kildare in the final.

"Above all, I will never forget lifting the Sam Maguire and carrying it across The Shannon. I don't cry very easily but I shed a tear on that Monday night after the final."

Re-locating from Waterford to Galway in 1973 didn't turn out to be a bad move for current County Board Secretary, John Power, who was transferred to the Western county during his service as a Garda. Four years into his role as secretary, John, originally from Ardmore in the Munster county, has seen at first hand the glory of winning a long-awaited All-Ireland title. John was previously P.R.O. of the Board for a number of years before being elected to his present role.

"It was a dream come true for me to be in Croke Park on All-Ireland final day. This win will show the rest of the country that Connacht football is now, at long last, at the very top. Any county in Connacht need not be afraid of any top teams in the rest of the country.

"The addition to the panel of a few younger players and the return of Kevin Walsh made a huge difference to the team. With so many young players, I certainly think they are capable of another All-Ireland.

"John O'Mahony, in leading Galway to the All-Ireland title, has brought new life back into Galway football. He is very focussed and meticulous in all his preparations for all games and he is now surely the top manager in the country.

"The Connacht championship, as always, will be very competitive but with Galway now the All-Ireland champions, every one of the other counties will be doing their utmost to try and dethrone us."

10

Route '98

It had to happen sometime, the golden years of another generation giving way to a vision of a Connacht team's dressingroom on All-Ireland final day again playing host to the Sam Maguire. Mayo's two close brushes with the elusive Gaelic chalice signalled the portent that such an event could happen before the Millennium. But few believed that when Galway took on Mayo in Castlebar and dethroned the defending provincial champions that an odyssey taking in Carrick-on-Shannon, Tuam and Roscommon along the way would conclude with the province's thirty two year famine at Croke Park banished in style.

The hazardous pursuit started with Galway giving the cold shoulder to the prospect of being beaten by Mayo for a third year running. A visit to Leitrim's own backyard followed before Galway were made to stare into the championship abyss in Tuam against Roscommon. Then, profiting from a goalkeeping mistake which forced the decisive goal in the provincial final replay, dismal Derry were dismissed in the Croke Park semi-final and next utopia, All-Ireland glory against Kildare, was Galway's. A province awestruck by a lavishly praised footballing resurgence, bathed in perfect happiness.

This is Galway's story 1998 - *Into The West* with Sam...

*   *   *   *

Connacht First Round:-

Galway.......... 1-13   Mayo.......... 2-6

Sunday, May 24th
At McHale Park, Castlebar
Attendance: 34,000.

For two summers Mayo had courted the brink of immortality. For two summers the West of Ireland expressed patriotic fervour that the province's Croke Park bogey on All-Ireland final day would come to an end. And for two summers long post-mortems and a pair of defeats had to be shouldered. Another winter endured, May 1998 arrived and with it came renewed optimism that this was the year the bogey would be broken. For a second year in succession the provincial open draw had pitted Mayo with Galway in the first round. To supporters of both counties this was a Connacht final in itself, an encounter with much recent history attached to the comprehensive pre-match hype it attracted. Galway had confidently won provincial honours in 1995, trouncing Mayo 0-17 to 1-7 in the final at Tuam. In 1996, roles were reversed when Mayo trumped Galway 3-9 to 1-11 in the final at Castlebar. And in 1997, Galway, courtesy of a slow start, were sent scrambling 1-16 to 0-15 by Mayo in a thrilling first round game at Tuam.

That broke Mayo's forty six year hoodoo at the North Galway venue and cost manager Val Daly his job. But one man's misfortune is often another man's fortune. Adding spice to Mayo-Galway 1998 was the fact that the Tribesmen were now under the guidance of John O'Mahony, the manager who brought Mayo to an All-Ireland final back in 1989. Live television coverage on *The Sunday Game* added to the occasion and for once Castlebar, with thirty four expectant spectators packed in, was the epicentre of the Gaelic footballing world. Two-and-a-half years Mayo had spent on the road in search of Sam but now, back on their home patch facing an eager-beaver Galway side, they were vulnerable.

And so it proved, but it was never easy. Galway, despite being in control during the second half, failed to put their opponents away and just five minutes remained when Mayo's Kieran McDonald was handed a chance to tie the scores. He somehow missed the point and there followed a sequence of Galway scores that wrapped up the four point win. Two goal chances had also gone abegging. On fifty seven minutes, McDonald was straight through on McNamara but the keeper saved, and on sixty minutes, he came in from the left-wing and shot ambitiously for a goal but the ball came crashing down off the crossbar and away to safety. A fine line had separated success and failure.

Manager O'Mahony deflected much credit for the victory away from himself but his motivational and tactical abilities to get the very best out of his players were on display for the seventy minutes. Apart from the wholesale positional switches that materialised after the ball was thrown in, the O'Mahony tactic which paid one of the richest dividends was designating John Divilly a free role. Along with negating the influence of Colm McMenamon, Divilly roamed the pitch, acting not only as a vital link man going forward but supplementing the defensive cover when needed. Time and again he was seen sending deliveries into Niall Finnegan and Padraic Joyce, both of whom made it a torrid afternoon for their markers, Kevin Cahill and Fergal Costello.

Another O'Mahony characteristic to the fore was his unperturbed calmness in the face of adversity. Midway through the first half, Galway had reached a crisis point. They trailed 1-5 to 0-4 and Mayo's eminence was palpably growing as McDonald had plundered the goal following a foolish short pass by goalkeeper Martin McNamara to no-one in particular. Other teams enduring a similar setback could well have folded at this juncture. But not Galway, not with the disciplined ethic O'Mahony had instilled in his charges. Galway's defence, sussing out the Mayo attack and firmly placing shackles on its influential operators, built up a head of steam which allowed them to draw level at 0-8 to 1-5 four minutes short of the break. There was still plenty of incident left as the half came to a close. There was a cracking goal from Derek Savage, created by Joyce after he gathered one of Divilly's long deliveries, along with McDonald's second goal for Mayo. But the pendulum had clearly swung back in favour of Galway, and in hindsight the scare they had overcome was to serve as a useful warning on how to cope with difficulties other summer days would pose.

Whereas both sets of forwards had been on top in the first thirty five minutes, Galway's defence, inspired by Ray Silke and Gary Fahy, gradually became an impenetrable fortress. Any decent Mayo move, which were few and far between in the second half, was broken down decisively. More powerful performers were midfield duo, Kevin Walsh and Seán Ó Domhnaill. The pair enjoyed great freedom as Mayo's Liam McHale was virtually anonymous and David Brady was unable to ignite any fire. So effective were Galway defensively that Mayo, who relied too heavily on the form of the erratic McDonald, managed just a solitary point in the second thirty five minutes. Not that Galway were profiting in attack, however. They managed just a solitary point in the opening twenty one minutes of the half. But then, following McDonald's rattling of the crossbar, they finally translated their control into scores. Finnegan, craftily bringing his experience to bear, had a hand in Galway's closing three points. First he was fouled and Joyce pointed. Finnegan himself pointed the next free and, indeed, he was fouled for the final free which he also pointed himself. The day was Galway's and deservedly so. Over the years, O'Mahony had rarely taken credit for success and Castlebar was no different. "This wasn't about me," divulged the manager afterwards. "This was about Galway, about the team and what they wanted. Whether or not I was around today, this game would have been won by Galway. It's as simple as that."

One hurdle overcome, a trip to Carrick-on-Shannon now concentrated the mind.

Galway: *Martin McNamara, Tomás Meehan, Gary Fahy, Tomás Mannion (0-1), Ray Silke, John Divilly, Seán Óg de Paor, Kevin Walsh, Seán Ó Domhnaill, Paul Clancy (0-1), Michael Donnellan, Jarlath Fallon (0-2, one free), Derek Savage (1-0), Padraic Joyce (0-4, three frees), Niall Finnegan (0-5, two frees). Subs. used: Declan Meehan for Clancy (50 mins), Tommy Joyce for Ó Domhnaill (70 mins).*

Mayo: *Peter Burke, Kenneth Mortimer, Kevin Cahill, Fergal Costello, David Heaney, James Nallen, Noel Connelly (0-1), Liam McHale, David Brady, David Nestor, Colm McMenamon, James Horan (0-1), Kieran McDonald (2-1), John Casey, Maurice Sheridan (0-3, one free). Subs. used: Kevin O'Neill for Horan (48 mins), Pat Holmes for Brady (57 mins), Ray Dempsey for Nestor (58 mins).*

Referee: *Eddie Neary (Sligo).*

*   *   *   *

Connacht Semi-Final:-

Galway.......... 1-16   Leitrim.......... 0-5

Sunday, June 14th
At Pairc Seán Mac Diarmada, Carrick-on-Shannon
Attendance: 12,000.

All through the three-week build-up to this semi-final, Galway manager John O'Mahony constantly stated that nothing ever came easy against Leitrim. In recent years, they had become an opposition to be reckoned with, in particular when O'Mahony himself managed them. One crunchy statistic keeping Galway on their toes was that Martin McNamara, Gary Fahy, Seán Óg de Paor, Damien Mitchell, Tomás Mannion, Kevin Walsh, Jarlath Fallon and Niall Finnegan were all on the side humbled in 1994, the year Leitrim won their breakthrough Connacht title.

Now under their latest manager, Fermanagh's Peter McGinnity, Leitrim's national league form tailored them as one of the country's top sixteen sides, something that was no mean achievement. In the end though, all Galway warnings guarding against complacency were misplaced as Leitrim, eccentrically putting on an abject display that was by far their worst in the championship for many a year, were desperate. Their five point return was, in all honesty, an embarrassment. Packed to the gills, Carrick-on-Shannon expected Leitrim to lay siege to Galway. Instead, without a whiff of championship fare in the air, Leitrim believers fast reappraised their hopes and with twenty minutes remaining they were trooping from the ground in their droves. Galway, enjoying the stroll in the summer sunshine, went on to seal the win with a late Finnegan goal.

Despite this, some observers departed wondering what good it had served Galway's provincial title hopes. There was no denying they possessed a slick batch of forwards who all had the beating of their Leitrim markers. Indeed, the full-forward line of Derek Savage, Finnegan and Padraic Joyce shared 1-12 between them. However the worry was that for so much control, why had it taken until practically the seventieth minute before the Leitrim net billowed? But that was a quandary best left for another day. The real question was what had happened to Leitrim. When Padraig McLoughlin reduced Galway's early lead to two points after fourteen minutes play, it signalled a reasonably close game was in the offing. But Leitrim, losing their way, did not score for another forty minutes. No single Leitrim defender lined out in the position in which he was selected, a tactic that caused confusion amongst their players further out the field. Was this done in an attempt to ward off the influence of O'Mahony who, having managed Leitrim previously, would have known all there was to know about their key players? Whatever, the switches failed and no Leitrim player was able to provide a spark to trigger some positive momentum. Instead, the negatives were everywhere to be seen.

For Galway, their display marked another chapter in the continuing evolution of Kevin Walsh and Seán Ó Domhnaill as a competent, twin peak midfield partnership. A high level of fielding, much physical presence, and quality distribution highlighted their contribution while in defence, Galway were equally effective. The half-back line of Ray Silke, John Divilly and Seán Óg de Paor looked unbeatable. Then again, the Leitrim forwards, suffering a severe case of stage-fright, never looked capable of causing trouble. Following McLoughlin's point, Galway stormed ahead. Revelling in yards of room and employing oodles of ideas, they reached the break ten points to two in front, with scores from Savage, Joyce and Finnegan, in particular, catching the eye.

Although Galway, as in the Mayo game, were held to only a point in the opening twenty minutes of the second half, the issue was never in doubt. Then, taking the initiative, corner-back Mannion roused Galway from their scoring slumber on fifty four minutes. Starting a move in his own half, he showed the intelligence to later offer support to Joyce and finish off the move. It broke the ice and three points in a three minute spell, from de Paor, Savage and Finnegan, followed. And that was that. Finnegan's goal, though well executed with a sidestep around goalkeeper Martin McHugh and a shot that squeezed passed Adrian Charles on the line, was academic.

Heady thoughts filled the minds of Galway's large travelling support. But manager O'Mahony was loaded with equanimity. Expressing impeccable politeness to his former Leitrim colleagues, he said: "My thoughts are with Leitrim. They did not justify the hard work that they put in during the winter, that was not a true reflection of their ability. We had that little bit of extra class that allowed us to take the scores."

Due recognition paid to his opponents, O'Mahony, with calculated foresight, was already looking ahead to the next day. "It was nice to get over this game and the victory was the important thing," he continued. "All I wanted out of today was a ticket to the Connacht final."

That ticket secured, Galway now took a back seat while Roscommon and Sligo got together to decide who would share the July 19th Tuam date.

Galway: *Martin McNamara, Tomás Meehan, Gary Fahy, Tomás Mannion (0-1), Ray Silke, John Divilly, Seán Óg de Paor (0-1), Kevin Walsh, Seán Ó Domhnaill, Paul Clancy (0-1), Michael Donnellan (0-1), Jarlath Fallon, Derek Savage (0-3), Padraic Joyce (0-5, two frees), Niall Finnegan (1-4, three frees). Subs. used: Declan Meehan for Clancy (52 mins), Tommy Joyce for Donnellan (65 mins), Damien Mitchell for Mannion (68 mins).*

Leitrim: *Martin McHugh, Adrian Charles, Derek Kelleher, Joe Tiffoney, Seamus Quinn (0-1), Shane McGettigan, Colin Regan, Pat Donohoe, Brendan Guckian, George Dugdale, Aidan Rooney, Fintan McBrien (0-2, both frees), Padraig McLoughlin (0-1), Adrian Cullen, Gene Bohan. Subs. used: Christopher Carroll for Guckian (34 mins), Liam Conlon (0-1) for Dugdale (half-time), Donal Brennan for Bohan (55 mins).*

Referee: *Sean McHale (Mayo).*

* * * *

Connacht Final:-

Galway.......... 0-11   Roscommon.......... 0-11

Sunday, July 19th
At Tuam Stadium, Tuam
Attendance: 26,000.

Heaving Tuam, soaked to the bone during an almighty deluge of heavy rain, balanced on a knife-edge. Two minutes remained and fourteen-man Roscommon were a point to the good. Galway, shaken by the tigerish running of their opponents, were staring into the championship abyss. Their forwards, dangling on the highwire with seventeen wides to their credit, were drowning in squandermania. And Roscommon, scenting victory admist the tense maelstrom, were on the attack once more. Another ball was sent slithering along the drenched surface towards their forwards, leaving Lorcan Dowd and Gary Fahy to grapple for possession twenty metres from goal. Fahy won the race but to many, it appeared that he had plucked the ball straight off the ground. Roscommon demanded a free to earn them a two point lead. Referee Seamus Prior blew his whistle, but instead of a Roscommon free Dowd was deemed to have fouled Fahy. It was the olive branch Galway needed. A pressure-relieving free later, Michael Donnellan won another face-saving free off Roscommon captain Clifford McDonald and Niall Finnegan, a jewel in adversity, pointed from thirty metres. With that, it was over. Galway, with backs no stranger to walls in the second half, had been that close to meltdown.

It was all a rude awakening for Galway, who appeared to have begun to believe the bloated hype being bandied around about them. Following their facile victory over Leitrim in the semi-final, Galway supporters, caught up in their own enthusiasm, had spoken as if they were already Connacht champions. True, on form after beating Leitrim and Mayo, no-one could genuinely say that either Roscommon or Sligo would pose a major obstacle. However, Roscommon, rediscovering confidence in their ability through a pair of late goals at Hyde Park, travelled to Markievicz Park and defiantly saw off Sligo with a commendable showing. In championship, it can often take one game, one win, to get a side low on confidence back in the reckoning. Roscommon now had two games under their belt and the positive feelings generated had them primed as underdogs clenched with a firm bite.

Not that this mattered to anyone. Galway were considered unbackable favourites, especially in their own Tuam Stadium. But, undeniably, that heavy weight of expectation took its toll on the players. Under pressure from a Roscommon side who had lost substitute Jason Neary within thirty seconds of his introduction on fifty minutes, Galway visibly struggled. While a question about their goal-scoring ability was asked of their forwards against Leitrim, the questions this time round were more cutting. Hoofing a colossal seventeen wides compared to Roscommon's four, some of Galway's shooting was unforgivable. Padraic Joyce missed a fourteen metre free near the interval. He also saw an earlier twenty five metre free come off an upright and Finnegan, equally fallible with the boot until late on, was also a prime contributor to the tally of wides. Their saving grace was their ailment had much to do with excellent blanket defending by Roscommon.

Another area where Galway's earlier championship eminence failed to materialise was midfield. Roscommon broke even, with Gerry Keane particularly prominent. Kevin Walsh and Seán Ó Domhnaill had shaded the battle in the first thirty five minutes but with much breaking ball being snapped up by Roscommon after the interval, Ó'Domhnaill was substituted early on and Jarlath Fallon was switched to a central role in an attempt to lessen the growing anxiety. It worked briefly, helping Galway establish a ten points to eight lead following Neary's impetuous departure, but it was never enough to win the match. No matter what Galway did, it was inadequate to shake off dogged Roscommon.

In the opening exchanges, Galway, playing into a stiff breeze, had the edge and established a four points to two lead after a quarter hour's play. It looked promising and when it was extended to six points to four by half-time they looked set fare. But they had not legislated for their squandermania to continue unabated in the second half. As for Roscommon, they were forced to live off scraps in the first half. With Galway defenders adapting better to conditions, Roscommon's erratic and predictable route-one tactic yielded little return. Their four scores all came from placed balls converted by Eddie Lohan. Nevertheless, they still managed to give Galway a pair of scares as goalkeeper Martin McNamara was forced to dive acrobatically to make goal-scoring saves to deny Dowd and Tommie Grehan.

Points from Fallon and Ó Domhnaill then put Galway ahead by double scores, eight points to four, shortly after the break. Roscommon were there for the taking but, changing tactics, they reeled off four unanswered points from play in just nine minutes to draw level. Roscommon were flying. Their half-back line, accurately hand-passing and attacking at will, swamped Galway's midfield and half-back line. But Fallon's switch helped combat the damage. Neary's dismissal for fouling Fallon helped even more and Galway, with points by Padraic and Tommie Joyce, re-established an even keel with ten minutes remaining. From here they looked winners, but Roscommon rallied again to move a point ahead. It was stirring stuff and Finnegan's free, which forced the replay, rescued Galway. And they even could have won it. However, Michael Donnellan's attempt to snatch it at the death sailed harmlessly wide.

Following all the hype from elsewhere beforehand, O'Mahony, in a bid to lessen that expectation, spent the post-mortem placing the replay onus firmly on Roscommon, especially as they were now at home in their Dr. Hyde Park enclave. As for those who anticipated Galway success at Tuam, O'Mahony stressed that he had said all week in the build-up that it was going to be close. "We had our chances but fair play to Roscommon, they were as good as I expected them to be. They were running at us and there was a situation towards the end that could have gone against us." Not that the manager had contemplated losing. "You never think of losing. Even when we went a point down all that was in my mind was getting a chance. And fair play to Finnegan. It wasn't a great day for free-takers but he did the business when he had to."

Replay looming though, more business remained to be done.

Galway: *Martin McNamara, Tomás Meehan, Gary Fahy, Tomás Mannion, Ray Silke, John Divilly, Seán Óg de Paor, Kevin Walsh, Seán Ó Domhnaill (0-1), Jarlath Fallon (0-2), Michael Donnellan, Declan Meehan (0-1), Derek Savage, Padraic Joyce (0-3, two frees), Niall Finnegan (0-3, all frees). Subs. used: Tommy Joyce (0-1) for Ó Domhnaill (48 mins), Shay Walsh for D. Meehan (60 mins).*

Roscommon: *Derek Thompson, Denis Gavin, Damien Donlon, Enon Gavin, Ciarán Heneghan, Clifford McDonald, Michael Ryan, Gerry Keane, Tom Ryan, Don Connellan, Fergal O'Donnell (0-1), Eddie Lohan (0-8, five frees, two '45s), Tommie Grehan (0-1), Nigel Dineen, Lorcan Dowd (0-1). Subs. used: Jason Neary (sent-off) for Keane (50 mins), Vinny Glennon for Grehan (61 mins).*

Referee: *Seamus Prior (Leitrim).*

*   *   *   *

Connacht Final Replay:-

Galway.......... 1-17   Roscommon.......... 0-17 (After Extra-Time)

Saturday, August 1st
At Dr. Hyde Park, Roscommon
Attendance: 28,000

Gripping was just one of many adjectives that tripped off the tongue following one hundred irresistible minutes of nerve-wracking, epic action. Just one goal, a score which stemmed from a goalkeeping error, separated the sides after extra-time but it was enough for Galway to announce their return to the big time Croke Park stage as Connacht champions. One central stream of thought had emanated from the Galway players following the draw in Tuam was that playing at Dr. Hyde Park would be more to their liking. It was. The pitch was in immaculate shape and the ball ran true. Trouble was, Dr. Hyde Park was also to Roscommon's liking and the near capacity crowd, enjoying the novelty of witnessing a Connacht provincial final on the August Bank Holiday Saturday, bubbled and bristled excitedly with every move.

Eight times the sides were level before the game's main headline was struck in bold in the opening seconds of the last period of extra-time. Jarlath Fallon's pointed effort dropped short and was collected by Derek Thompson. Under pressure from three Galway players, Niall Finnegan, Shay Walsh and Michael Donnellan, the goalkeeper, who had been performing with distinction, went across his goal and in the process of making a hand-pass, spilled the ball which was subsequently dispatched to the net by the lurking Donnellan. In a stroke, Galway's voyage of discovery was embellished. Now five points in front, nothing, not even a valiant attempted comeback by Roscommon, could prevent John O'Mahony from managing a third Connacht team to a provincial title.

Galway had learned from their near nemesis in Tuam. They showed they had developed character and again, they possessed the patience not to panic when things were not going their way. The tricky situation they found themselves in this time was trailing Roscommon ten points to eight with eleven minutes remaining. But they possessed the resolve not only to equalise but to go in front and they left Roscommon relying upon a last ditch equaliser to force extra-time. On it went and the intensity of the unstinting effort only lost its edge in pace in the closing stages when Galway looked winners. It was a marvellous testament to both teams and come September, with All-Ireland honours pocketed, the real value of this two-game instalment with Roscommon was fully appreciated by Galway.

Plus points for O'Mahony were the improved displays by Fallon, Donnellan and Seán Óg de Paor. Fallon, despite early erratic shooting, found the range in the plentiful space he was afforded by picking off five scores from play. Donnellan's pace and movement was problematic all afternoon. Switched from centre-forward to the right wing, he was at the hub of every Galway move and his electric speed was a constant thorn. And tireless de Paor, who raided down the left flank at every opportunity and reaped two good scores for his efforts, had a stormer. The three were Galway's most prominent players and their eminence was badly needed as the provincial champions left Dr. Hyde Park knowing that they had nearly shot themselves in the foot again with a tally of twenty wides compared to Roscommon's thirteen. Another problem was that Galway, still seeking a reliable half-forward partner for Donnellan and Fallon to replace the injured Paul Clancy, were left disappointed as Tommie Joyce, starting in place of Declan Meehan, failed to shine and was substituted on forty nine minutes.

Forward frailties aside though, Galway had much to be happy with. While Roscommon had broken even in Tuam, Kevin Walsh and Seán Ó Domhnaill shaded the midfield battle here. Gerry Keane had some good moments and Tom Ryan ran himself into the ground but was not as prominent as expected. The Galway duo meanwhile provided a good platform for their forward line for most of the game and the fact that Galway won every throw-in was indicative of the exchanges in this area. Walsh's injury however, sustained ten minutes from the end of extra-time, was a cause for concern. Elsewhere, Galway's blanket defending was a notable feature, leading to a lot of Roscommon movement breaking down due to enforced over-elaboration. Ray Silke, following an edgy opening marking Eddie Lohan, benefited from the enforced restructuring that saw the concussed John Divilly called ashore on thirty minutes to be replaced by Damien Mitchell. And Gary Fahy, uncomfortable at times under high dropping balls, wielded enough influence to force Roscommon's Nigel Dineen to forage deeper out the field.

Five points to four Galway had led at the normal half-time break and points by Derek Savage and de Paor shortly after the restart put some daylight between the protagonists. However, it did not last long and with Galway scoring just once in the following twenty one minutes, Roscommon, aided by four points from play, found themselves two ahead. Briefly,

Galway looked troubled but Finnegan, rising to the occasion, slotted ove
two scores to tie matters up and de Paor, counter-attacking once more, stol
a lead two minutes short of the final whistle. It looked as if Galway wer
through but Lohan, as Finnegan had done in the drawn game, popped ove
a pressure free to finish it at eleven points all, a full-time score that mirrore
Tuam. Extra-time saw Galway reach the interval two points ahead. /
Roscommon surge was expected but Thompson's mistake stalled that rall
and gave Galway the breathing space that was to usher captain Silke up t
receive the silverware afterwards. Galway were provincial champions an
the emotion of the achievement was not lost on O'Mahony. "I'm delighte
on behalf of Galway," he gushed outside the dressingrooms in a brief displa
of emotion. "They showed great character when they went two points down
There was a lot of things said about our team in the last fortnight since th
drawn game. There was expectancy probably from some people but there'
a lot of kids out there and that's the way I look at them. There was a lot o
learning to do but it was unreal expectation and we came and did a lot o
learning out there on the field today," he said trumpeting the absorbe
lessons of Dr. Hyde Park. "Obviously we got the break of the goal and tha
gave us a cushion and once the workrate was there, we closed it out an
didn't do anything silly."

Silly was Roscommon's forte alone, a single mistake had undone thei
ambitions. Next up for Galway, Derry at Croke Park.

Galway: *Martin McNamara, Tomás Meehan, Gary Fahy, Tomás Mannion
Ray Silke, John Divilly, Seán Óg de Paor (0-2), Kevin Walsh, Seán Ó Domhnaill
Jarlath Fallon (0-5), Michael Donnellan (1-3, one free, one '45), Tommy Joyce
Derek Savage (0-3), Padraic Joyce (0-1), Niall Finnegan (0-2, one free). Subs
used: Damien Mitchell for Divilly (31 mins), Shay Walsh (0-1) for T. Joyce (5?
mins), Fergal Gavin for Walsh (90 mins).*

Roscommon: *Derek Thompson, Denis Gavin, Damien Donlon, Enon Gavin
Ciarán Heneghan, Clifford McDonald, Michael Ryan, Gerry Keane,Tom Ryan
Don Connellan, Fergal O'Donnell (0-2), Eddie Lohan (0-8, six frees, one '45)
Tommie Grehan (0-2), Nigel Dineen (0-3), Lorcan Dowd (0-1). Subs. used
Derek Duggan for Grehan (65 mins), Vinny Glennon (0-1) for T. Ryan (80 mins)
Tommie Grehan for Duggan (90 mins).*

Referee: *Seamus Prior (Leitrim).*

*   *   *   *

All-Ireland Semi-Final:-

Galway.......... 0-16   **Derry 1-8**

Sunday, August 23rd
At Croke Park, Dublin
Attendance: 38,569.

John O'Mahony's parting shot following the replay success at Dr. Hyde Park was that his side still had much to learn. Although equipped with an arsenal of silky forward skills to create frequent scoring chances, Galway had fast developed a propensity to waste a whopping chunk of that good approach play. Solve that problem and there would be no stopping them was the popular theory. Against Derry, that problem was emphatically solved.

Derry's late penalty goal left the final score looking much closer than it really was as Galway, portraying slick potency, had only three wides, none of them from play. Granted nine of Galway's sixteen point total resulted from frees, but the scoring of such a high tally of frees served perfectly to illustrate how poor Derry were. Short of inspiration and organisation, it was cringing at times to witness the inept mistakes they made. A lack of common sense mystified even more. Corner-backs and brothers, Kieran and Emmett McKeever, were one pair who persisted in the concession of a surfeit of frees. So regular were the infringements that Kieran, the captain, was eventually sent off in the fifty first minute for a foul on Michael Donnellan. And what made Derry's demise even more unpalatable was that they retired at the interval six points down they remerged for the second half without a change, not even a positional one.

It was strange stuff, but Galway were not complaining. They took control from the first whistle and never allowed Derry's trademark passing to sustain any rhythm. While Padraic Joyce put little astray with the free-taking, Jarlath Fallon sparkled with some scintillating scores. Disregarding the team ethic, Fallon showed he was one of those rare breeds - possessing good shooting, firm tackling, accurate passing, lively pace, feisty power, solid presence and disciplined temperament - the complete Gaelic footballer. Another to leave an indelible impression was Donnellan whose zip and zest in the chase for possession gave Galway a foundation on which they were not to flounder. Yet again, the midfield pairing of Kevin Walsh and Seán Ó Domhnaill flourished. Until the Wednesday prior to the game Walsh, recovering from his Connacht final replay injury, had been a major doubt. But any worry was quickly extinguished when the midfielder, in his own square, rose to gather Anthony Tohill's early free.

Galway's defence were also in sublime form. Seán Óg de Paor again revelled in his attacking role while Ray Silke, elected as the man with the free role when McKeever was sent-off, intelligently used the space it afforded. That alone showed Galway were on an upward learning curve as they had struggled previously in Tuam against fourteen-man Roscommon. But the paradox about Galway being so good was that they were still made to rely upon goalkeeper Martin McNamara to make three excellent saves to keep his colleagues' lead intact. Of all people, Joe Brolly, Derry's goal-scoring winner in the Ulster final, bore down on him on thirty nine minutes but McNamara was swiftly off his line to smoother the effort. Next, with an hour gone, Tohill, another of Derry's reputation-carrying players, was upended and appealed for a penalty. Play continued and in the ensuing commotion the ball ran to substitute Joe Cassidy whose point-blank shot was blocked by McNamara. Then Geoffrey McGonigle tried his luck against the Corofin net-minder, but to no avail. Only the penalty, procured for a foul on Eamon Burns and taken by Coleman, went past McNamara. He had portrayed a joyous defiance.

In the past, Connacht teams had made tentative starts at Croke Park and before they realised it their opponents had the winning of the game. No apprehension was evident in Galway as O'Mahony, shrewdly motivating his charges, instilled an all-encompassing clinical detachment and will-to-win. Avoiding the emotional involvement that can cloud the mind, little was to undermine the players' footballing technique. A dozen minutes elapsed and Galway found themselves four unanswered points to the good. Relaxing, they allowed Derry a modicum of possession to take the next three scores but there was to be no equaliser. Rattling off five in a row (four frees and a point from play by Joyce) the half-hour mark saw them enter a comfort zone and the interval arrived with Galway ten points to four ahead.

Then, as in the Mayo and Leitrim games, their habit of slowly starting the second half again arose. It took nearly a quarter of an hour for them to register a score but it was not a major concern. Derry only managed three points in that period and once McKeever had trudged to the sideline Galway's success was sealed and delivered. Joyce and Fallon shared points before Fallon sanctioned the coup-de-grace, banging over a delicious left-footed point in an instant reply to Coleman's consolation penalty.

Stylish and assured with no unnecessary passing, Galway had provided the perfect antidote to Derry's dreariness. O'Mahony, for once, concurred in an incisive appraisal of the afternoon's events. "There was good closing down today. The modern game is all about that and we did that well. There's a lot of good things about this team and pace is one. We tried to utilise our strengths." As in the aftermath of previous games, the next day was already on the manager's mind. "It's a learning experience. There is still an awful lot of improving to be done. We're in an All-Ireland final and that's all we could ask at this stage. Nice to sit back and relax and get ready for the final."

Only eight teams from the West had contested an All-Ireland final since the province's last win in 1966. Now Galway's qualification, progress which gave Connacht football a third successive final appearance, emphasised blossoming credentials in the game's upper echelons. The fateful day to fulfil potential was now to hand.

Galway: *Martin McNamara, Tomás Meehan, Gary Fahy, Tomás Mannion, Ray Silke, John Divilly, Seán Óg de Paor, Kevin Walsh, Seán Ó Domhnaill (0-1), Fergal Gavin, Michael Donnellan (0-2, both frees), Jarlath Fallon (0-4), Derek Savage, Padraic Joyce (0-8, six frees), Niall Finnegan (0-1). Sub. used: Shay Walsh for Gavin (51 mins).*

Derry: *Eoin McCloskey, Kieran McKeever (sent-off), Sean Martin Lockhart, Emmet McKeever, Paul McFlynn (0-1), Henry Downey, Gary Coleman (1-1, penalty goal), Anthony Tohill, Enda Muldoon, Gary Magill, Dermot Dougan, Eamonn Burns (0-3, two frees), Joe Brolly, Seamus Downey, Enda Gormley (0-2, both frees). Subs. used: Joe Cassidy (0-1) for Brolly (44 mins), Dermot Heaney for Magill (46 mins), Geoffrey McGonigle for Dougan (65 mins).*

Referee: *John Bannon (Longford).*

*   *   *   *

All-Ireland Final:-

Galway.......... 1-14   Kildare.......... 1-10

Sunday, September 28th
At Croke Park, Dublin
Attendance: 65,886.

This was the day the myth that Connacht football had been in terminal decline was finally shown up for the folly that it was. Galway, majestically unveiling a brand of Gaelic that revisited the hallowed corridors of the catch and kick academy, went down into history as one of the few teams to have ever won Sam Maguire in magnificent fashion. Snatches of their powerful and direct football were shown in the game's opening quarter, but their opening salvo following the interval was simply breathtaking. Tactically, they were the more versatile side and a goal and four points signalled an unbreakable foundation for victory. Kildare, short on ideas, were ruffled.

All-Ireland finals had often left room for argument and debate over whether a side deserved its success. No such post mortems hindered Galway as they lapped up the generous plaudits. And deservedly so. Kildare's preoccupation with the short hand-passing game was no match for a Galway outfit adorned with better forwards. The Lilywhites, unable to react as the game evolved, failed to realise that a goal and six of their total materialised from playing direct balls in on top of the Galway defence. That potential to hurt Galway was never fully utilised and Kildare could have no qualms come the finish. Tomás Meehan subdued Padraic Graven, Gary Fahy rendered Karl O'Dwyer increasingly anonymous and Tomás Mannion, a smooth operator who sent Martin Lynch packing to an ignominious substitution, all played their part. Their intelligent play helped make Galway winners. In attack, the forwards, playing to their strengths, made regular scoring inroads on Kildare. The enthusiasm of prodigious Michael Donnellan, Jarlath Fallon's subtle ball-juggling and the eagerness of their full-forward line all attributed to Kildare's failure to grapple with the questions asked by Galway of their outlandish pre-match hype, a hype based on victories over the three previous All-Ireland winners - Dublin, Meath and Kerry.

Not that it was all plain-sailing. Galway, neglecting the football that had initially worked for them, resorted to a nightmare version of Kildare's short-passing game. Dawdling in possession, the tactic led to little but confusion and frustration and it allowed Kildare to quickly scupper Galway's early advantage. Eddie McCormack's opening score was soon followed by Dermot Earley's palmed goal. The move stemmed from some pressure play by Lynch who released Willie McCreery for the killer pass to Earley and when Karl O'Dwyer knocked over the next score, alarm bells began to chime. Kildare's key figures had started to exert themselves. Their midfield, McCreery and Niall Buckley, were ascendant over Kevin Walsh and Seán Ó Domhnaill and Galway were struggling. But for all their possession Kildare failed to reap when time was ripe. A four point lead was the best they could muster, 1-5 to 0-4, and Padraic Joyce's point just short of the interval to leave only a score in it gave Galway a vital psychological boost.

Strategy tweaked, they returned for the second half intent on getting their direct game back on track. With a vengeance, they attacked Kildare who froze in the early Galway flurry. Three minutes into the half, a five man move ended with Fallon landing a beautifully angled score. It settled Galway. They now saw Kildare were there for the taking. More importantly, the point settled Fallon who was out-of-sorts in the first half. Playing with confidence restored, the centre-forward's display was unrelenting in its potency and the sublime delivery of a forty metre sideline over the crossbar was the stuff dreams are made of. Equally of the dream-like mould was Galway's thirty ninth minute goal. John Divilly won a free and drove it long down the field to Donnellan who slipped a well-timed pass inside to Joyce. Time stood still as Joyce shaped to shoot but instead of belting the ball past Christy Byrne, he calmly danced round him and finished to the empty net. In one sweeping move, Galway had sight of Sam Maguire.

Further scores flowed, with Finnegan (two) and Fallon (one) pulling the strings while the Galway defence were impervious. Divilly, after a dubious start, controlled his patch, while the leg-pumping de Paor was as impressive in the execution of his defensive duties as he was in his sallies forward. Even the troubled midfield assumed an aura of invincibility and Ó Domhnaill's fifty fourth minute long-range point indicated that Galway were in complete control. Kildare chased the game but Galway, unlike previous collapses in other seasons, stood firm. Leinster hopes hinged on substitute Pauric Brennan, who scored three points during his twenty six minutes on the pitch. But, in truth, a goal was needed and another substitute, Brian Murphy, nearly provided it. As the game lurched into added time, his flick-on of a long delivery shaved the outside of a post. Pressure continued to mount and Earley managed a point to leave only a goal between the sides. But Galway were not to be denied. Just as they had done in reply to a late Derry score in the semi-final, Galway paraded their incisiveness one final time. It was another example of anything Kildare could do, Galway could do better. And fittingly it was de Paor, making up the ground, who was the beneficiary, finishing off with a point following quick ball up the field by substitute Paul Clancy, Silke, Fallon and Donnellan.

The images afterwards were to be treasured. Galway supporters, many occupying the Canal End terrace for the last time before its demolition for a new stand, swamped the pitch in a whirlpool outpouring of raw emotion. Silke's oration banished memories of bad old days and 'The Fields of Athenry' was given a rousing rendition. The importance the breakthrough signified was best left to the liberator, John O'Mahony to sum up. "It's fantastic for Galway to bring back the All-Ireland title after so many years but this team are at the end of a period in which Connacht football has gone through a real transformation and every county in their own way has played their part in this success," he enthused. "There has been a rising tide and I think we have been at the end of it and reaped the rewards of many."

It was now reality. A thirty two year generation gap had, at last, been surmounted and as sweet a summer one could ever imagine had ended smelling of well-deserved success. Sam was finally going *Into The West*...!

Galway: *Martin McNamara, Tomás Meehan, Gary Fahy, Tomás Mannion, Ray Silke, John Divilly, Seán Óg de Paor (0-2), Kevin Walsh, Seán Ó Domhnaill (0-1), Shay Walsh, Michael Donnellan (0-2), Jarlath Fallon (0-3, one sideline), Derek Savage, Padraic Joyce (1-2, one free), Niall Finnegan (0-4, two frees). Sub. used:Paul Clancy for Walsh (66 mins).*

Kildare: *Christy Byrne, Brian Lacey, John Finn, Ken Doyle, Sos Dowling, Glen Ryan, Anthony Rainbow, Niall Buckley (0-1), Willie McCreery, Eddie McCormack (0-2), Declan Kerrigan (0-1), Dermot Earley (1-1), Martin Lynch, Karl O'Dwyer (0-2), Padraig Graven. Subs. used: Pauric Brennan (0-3, two frees) for Graven (46 mins), Brian Murphy for Lynch (58 mins).*

Referee: *John Bannon (Longford).*